ARSETROLOGY

ARSETROLOGY

How your poo can predict your future

Harry Holland
with
Oliver Scheidt

piatkus

PIATKUS

First published in Great Britain in 2009 by Piatkus

A CIP catalogue record for this book is available from the British Library

ISBN 978-0-7499-4027-0

Typeset in Bliss and Futura
Printed and bound in Great Britain by Clays Ltd, St Ives plc

Papers used by Piatkus are natural, renewable and recyclable products sourced
from well-managed forests and certified in accordance with the rules of the
Forest Stewardship Council.

Mixed Sources
Product group from well-managed
forests and other controlled sources
www.fsc.org Cert no. SGS-COC-004081
© 1996 Forest Stewardship Council
FSC

Piatkus
An imprint of
Little, Brown Book Group
100 Victoria Embankment
London EC4Y 0DY

An Hachette UK Company
www.hachette.co.uk

www.piatkus.co.uk

Contents

Acknowledgements

Thanks to:

Laura, for listening to my shit jokes.
Rob, for great advice throughout the whole process.
Helen, for guiding this strange concoction into the light.
And my dear old mum, who must be so proud of what her little
boy's doing with his life.

Harry Holland

This book could not have been written without the hard work
of my diligent researchers at the University of Waterloo: the
excellent Jonathan Brown and his lovely fiancé, Elizabeth Trout.
My sincere thanks and best wishes for the wedding. I do hope
you've abandoned your ill-conceived plan to hyphenate your
surnames; trust me: no good can come of it.

Oliver Scheidt

Introduction

Welcome to *Arsetrology*, a beginners' guide to the incredible world of colonic interpretation. For those who don't know — and that's probably most of you — colonic interpretation is a long-forgotten[1] system of fortune-telling based on something that everybody on the planet does every single day. Namely, have a poo.

At this point, we'd better get over the nervous sniggering that seems inevitable whenever anyone mentions the toilet or what goes on there. Go on, have a chuckle about it. Nobody's judging you. We'll just wait here until you're finished. In fact, let's help you get this out of your system (so to speak). For, no matter how normal a part of everyday life it might be, it is an undeniable truth that the various euphemisms and epithets for the very natural act of passing a stool are both numerous and frequently hilarious.

Therefore, ladies and gentlemen, in an effort to help you come to terms with your natural but regrettable tendency to giggle childishly whenever this subject is raised, we give you the glory that is crap — or poo, plop, shit, shite, turd, bog, stools, kaka, number two, gut mud, tummy fruit, jobbies, the brown trout, the brown mouse, the tortoise's head, arse chocolate, dookie, do-dos and bum eggs, to name but a few.

That takes care of the Beast itself, but what about the Unspeakable Act? Glad you asked, because we've all felt the urge to have a shit, take a crap, have a dump, touch cloth, drop the kids off at the pool, back one out, open the bomb bay doors, drop a depth charge, punish the porcelain, bomb the bowl, damage the drain, drop a log, lay a cable, launch a torpedo, build a log cabin, release the hostages, coil some rope, pinch a loaf, make some fudge, lose a farting contest, drop anchor, take a squat, grow a tail, test the plumbing, bring out the heavy artillery or unload some cargo.

---

[1] And some might say deservedly so.

Truly a bewildering array of overly descriptive but undeniably amusing terms – and that's without plumbing the depths[2] of the hundred-and-one hideous ways to describe diarrhoea.

So: all done? Good.

Because the fact of the matter (and we use the word 'fact' quite incorrectly) is that this sniggering is what prevents you from seeing into the future. We've just explored some very good (and, quite frankly, extremely inventive) reasons why most people giggle whenever the utterly natural act of crapping is mentioned – but why the discomfort? Is it shame, embarrassment or squeamishness? No. It's fear. Most people are *scared* of the toilet, because when you're on the toilet all your social niceties fall away and you're just another animal squeezing a turd out of your anus.

In purely mechanical terms, backing one out is the very natural end product of the process by which we fuel our bodies, but this simple act is affected by all sorts of factors. What you excrete is the product not just of body, but of body, mind and spirit. It is, in fact, a condensed slice of destiny, right there in your toilet bowl.

That's why this book exists – to help you understand the incredible forces at work every single time you take a dump. There are plenty of books you can *read* on the toilet, but very few of them (with the exception of a few diet books and one or two specialist Dutch publications) deal with what actually *takes place* on the toilet. And none of them – *none of them* – broach the spiritual aspects of excretion.

So get over your hang-ups and take a moment to listen to what your body is trying to tell you. You may be surprised at what you learn.[3]

---

[2] Sorry, but you might as well get used to it from the start.

[3] Although our preliminary research indicates that 'horrified' may be nearer the mark.

Disclaimer

The authors would like to point out that they have no qualifications, no firm grip on reality and absolutely no idea what they're talking about. The diagnoses, strategies and suggestions offered in this book are made purely for comic effect, and are frequently inaccurate, often impractical and occasionally dangerous. Anybody stupid enough actually to listen to a word we say shouldn't come crying to us if they find out that following the advice herein has ruined their life.

Really. We did warn you.

How To Use This Book

OK, right off the bat let's get one thing clear: you are not expected or encouraged to touch anything from the toilet bowl. Toilet reading works on observation – not handling – of stools, so keep your hands out of the danger zone.

If you can remember that basic rule, you're pretty much qualified to begin your journey into the arcane practice of Arsetrology. Needless to say, it's a good idea to keep this book close to the toilet. Leaving it on a bookshelf in the lounge would require much to-ing and fro-ing, not to mention the readying of some seriously inventive explanations for when your guests ask what the hell you're doing. So best keep it by the lavvy.

Rather than examine each individual poo strand, the process of identification has been simplified into forty-five runes that allow for quick identification and interpretation. The complete set can be seen between Pages 10 and 14.

Compare what you've produced to the table of Rectal Runes and then turn to the page indicated above the diagram. There you'll find a **Quick Reading**, which gives you the basic gist of the manifestation and how it relates to your past, present and future. This is essentially the 'fortune cookie' version of the reading (if that isn't too disgusting an idea) and tells you what you need to know in a nutshell. This is here in case you don't have time to read the full interpretation. Also included in this quick assessment are several variables that can affect the reading. To understand the first of these, it's worth repeating the old maxim used by proctologists and ITV sitcom writers alike:

When you produce shit, it's all about consistency.

With that in mind, we must consider not only the shape of your poo, but also the manner in which it's produced – the **Rites of**

Passage, as it were. If it emerges **Calm & Serene** (that is, gently and without a fight) it is considered a good omen and this has a positive bearing on your future. However, if your turd arrives full of **Sound & Fury**, your body is producing negative karma and that means some very bad mojo. The two lists indicate the two extreme ends of what can happen when this rune appears in the bowl and offer further insight into what's in store.

There is, of course, another major variable that can affect the manifestation of a rune. The **What Did You Eat?** section seeks to provide some guidance as to whether your diet may have played some role in the formation of your stool, or whether Mr Ploppy's bizarre shape is purely a manifestation of karmic forces. Sometimes, we'll speculate on which diet would be applicable if the rune in question were to take on a physical manifestation. There's no sound Arsetrological reason for this, but we get bored easily and it's good for a laugh.

The **Detailed Reading** goes through all the facets of the rune and offers further insights. If you really want to understand what's happening, you'll want to read this in full. Don't dismiss it if the relevance doesn't immediately hit you. Once you've been immersed in the world of Arsetrology for a while, you'll realise that everything can change once you wipe, stand up and flush.

Of course, after assimilating all of this information, you'll no doubt want to know what you should do. **What Action Can I Take?** is the section to help you with this dilemma. We must repeat at this stage that you follow our suggestions at your own peril. We will generally seek to give you some *ideas* that might prove helpful, but, without knowing the exact nature of (a) your crap and (b) your personal situation, we are in no position to advise you with any degree of accuracy. We seek only to provide you with the tools to interpret your turds – what you do with that knowledge is entirely your own business.

It's not uncommon for people to have difficulty in coming to terms with this extraordinary knowledge. We are not all of us immediately at home with arcane practices and it can take some time to accept this fresh way of looking at the world. In order to help ground your new insights in reality, as you have been used to it, we've also provided some **Historical Context**. This is designed to help you see how famous figures from history might have coped with each rune.

Finally, since Arsetrology is art as much as a science, we felt that we should deal with the very real possibility that some of these runes won't necessarily land in exactly the position in which you see them on the page. In this case, it's up to you, as the observer, to decide whether your shit is just a little off centre, stuck at right angles or drifting clockwise. Sometimes it will be so out of alignment as to be considered almost upside down. For those who find themselves in this situation, we have provided the **Inverted** section to help you interpret what is very often effectively a completely different rune. Good luck with that.

And that's pretty much it. We hope you enjoy what you learn on the toilet and encourage you to share the knowledge with others. Together, we can overcome people's fears and open up their hearts and minds[4] to the mysteries of the ages. As the Roman philosopher Shittius Maximus — widely regarded as the first real Arsetrologer — famously remarked: *Meus excretum vultus amo an barrus. Quis operor vos volo ut opes?*[5]

---

[4] And, of course, their bottoms. You didn't think we were going to pass that one up, did you?

[5] Loosely translated: 'Hey! My shit looks like an elephant. What do you suppose that means?'

The Rectal Runes

Use this section as a quick reference to guide you to the detailed readings later in the book. Remember that this process is as much art as science, so the rune does not have to be an exact match to what you've produced. It's up to you, the reader (and, indeed, shitter) to correctly interpret your mess.

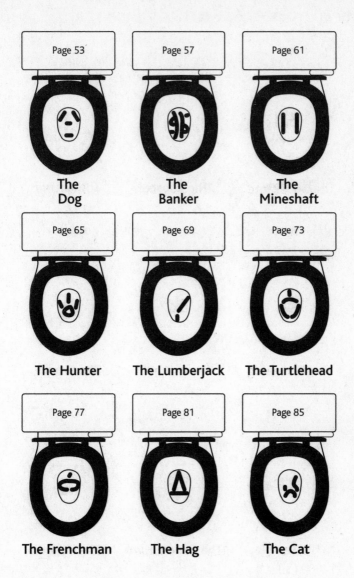

The
Dog
Page 53

The
Banker
Page 57

The
Mineshaft
Page 61

The Hunter
Page 65

The Lumberjack
Page 69

The Turtlehead
Page 73

The Frenchman
Page 77

The Hag
Page 81

The Cat
Page 85

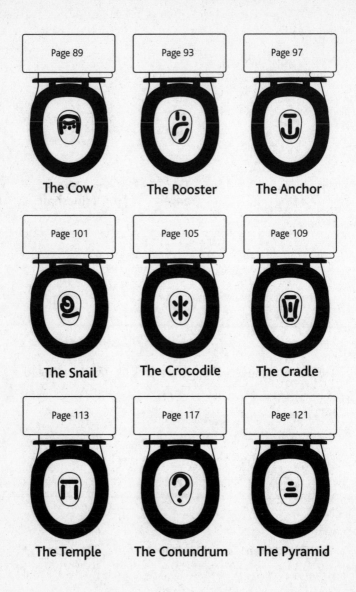

The Readings

Use this section to gain insight into the manifestations, using the notes in the introduction if necessary. You are advised to read the full interpretation, even if it doesn't initially seem relevant. There are many hidden meanings that will become clear after a full reading. If this doesn't prove to be the case, the problem very clearly lies with you and your woeful inability to read poo correctly, despite our detailed and foolproof tutelage. Try harder.[6]

---

[6] Not *too* hard, though, lest you're struck with piles. Arse grapes are no fun, believe us.

The Debutante

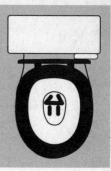

Quick Reading

Everyone likes to make a splash on arrival, but be careful not to be *too* showy. You never get a second chance to make a first impression.

 Rites of Passage

Calm & Serene

Ah, the relief! You're easing into a new social scene with barely a ripple to mark your passing. New friends accept you as if you'd always been there, and you're free to explore these uncharted social waters without fear of rejection.

Sound & Fury

Oh dear! You've made a splash, all right; in fact, you're your own worst enema. Remember that dream you used to have as a child? The one where you went to school in your pyjamas, or, worse still, naked? We bet you wish you felt that comfortable, now.

What Did You Eat?

At the risk of stating the bleeding obvious,[7] The Debutante is a very particular and regimented rune, consisting, as it does, of five straight lines. It must be clear – even to somebody dim enough to be sitting on the bog, trying to chart a course through life by studying their own shit – that this is not natural. Armed with this knowledge, we can quickly ascertain The Debutante's relevance to us.

---

[7] Please note that this is strictly a figure of speech – if what you've left in the bowl is obviously bleeding, we urge you to seek medical attention.

If your diet consists mainly of organic vegetables and lentil casserole, then clearly passing a rune of such rigidity is extremely unlikely and should be treated as the omen it is: take the interpretations in this section very seriously. If, on the other hand, your dietary regimen comprises lots of straight – or straight-ish – morsels that could easily form some kind of frame or splint for crap to accrete to (like shin splints, if you like – but one letter off), then there's probably a more scientific explanation for your plop. And you should give some thought to chewing, rather than inhaling, your Twiglets in future.

Detailed Reading

This is an exciting time for you, as you meet new people, go to new places and have experiences that you never previously thought possible. Like a social butterfly emerging from the chrysalis of solitude, you're ready to break out onto a new social scene. Or, on the other hand, you're paralysed by fear of your strange new surroundings – annoyingly vague, this telling-the-future shit, isn't it?

The main thing to bear in mind is that you are entering a time of change and you need to think about making some adjustments. Remember when you reluctantly had to leave behind those carefree schooldays to enter the workforce as a (so-called) productive member of society? We're betting you had to make some pretty drastic changes in those heady days, and now you need to draw upon those memories and once again embrace the changes coming your way.

If you interpret your rune correctly and act on your findings, the path is clear to move into a bright new future. What you do there is up to you, but make the most of this new opportunity you've been given – second chances don't come along every day.

🧻 What Action Can I Take?

The essence of this rune is that it's a sign of change; and how you respond to change very much depends on whether you're excited to be trying something new or frightened to be leaving your comfort zone.

If you embrace change and find yourself eager to try something new, the only thing you really have to do is try to keep a level head (looking at the ruler-straight lines of The Debutante, it's clear that you've already got a very level arse, so that's a nice start). But if you fear change – and, really, that's by far the most common cause of this particular rune – then you have some work ahead of you to see it off. You could try prying your bumhole open and wiggling your botty over the toilet in an effort to produce fat, curly plops rather than the thin, rigid lines of The Debutante – but that's (a) addressing the symptom rather than the cause, and (b) pretty disgusting.

🏛 Historical Context

Marie Antoinette is the classic archetypal Debutante. There can be few more impressive debuts than to be presented as consort to the Dauphin of France, the future Louis XVI, secure in the knowledge that – barring disease (possible, but much less likely for the aristocrats than the peasants) or revolution (ah, now there's a funny thing . . .) – you will one day be queen of the French.

All well and good, but what does this have to do with poo? Well, there are two key points to consider.

First, her famous response to the news that the peasants had no bread – 'let them eat cake' – was a recipe for less-than-healthy botty products if ever we heard one; and, second,

The Debutante

she was executed by guillotine, and who among us hasn't sat on our throne, straining away to produce a turd through a ring piece reduced to the size of a Frenchman's courage, and thought, 'Fuck this for a laugh – I wish someone would just cut my head off and put me out of my misery'?

Inverted

There is a charming symmetry to the inversion of The Debutante. In its original state, it is all straight lines and grace, very like its namesake, but, inverted, it becomes . . . well, there's no getting away from it: it's two fingers up at the world, isn't it? While The Debutante offers you a hand to be taken by the fingers and kissed, the inverted Debutante offers two fingers and tells you to kiss its arse. Nice.

The Quagmire

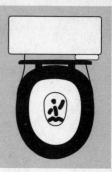

Quick Reading

Something stinks here – be careful not to get bogged down in a mess you can't get out of.

♌ Rites of Passage

Calm & Serene

Although it may not be much fun to have your boot stuck in the peat, it's worth remembering that quagmires are a vital part of the ecology. That said, if you find any tiny life forms inhabiting *this* particular swamp, you may want to consider cleaning your loo. For a change.

Sound & Fury

Whether the word is used literally or figuratively, it can be very difficult to disentangle yourself from a quagmire. That terrible sinking feeling you've got is not to be ignored!

🍔 What Did You Eat?

Despite the ancient origins of The Quagmire – it being a reminder of the primordial ooze from which we all came – the rune itself has become increasingly prevalent in the modern age. There's currently some debate as to the cause of these elevated numbers of Quagmires. Some view it as symbolic of the modern age – an Arsetrological reflection of a collective subconscious trapped in a self-perpetuating cycle of consumption and waste. Others think it's due to the rise of organic fruit and veg and the fact that we're paying through the nose for wonky carrots that are covered in shit.

And the sunflower-seed dieticians tell you that you're not even supposed to wash the things, because 'that's where all the nutrients are'. It's where the germs are, too, so, if you've bought into the organic-veg conspiracy, it may well account for the mucky stuff floating in your toilet bowl.

 Detailed Reading

OK, so you've inadvertently stepped in something wet and smelly. Ordinarily, this would be no big problem – you'd simply wipe your shoes on a patch of grass and be on your way. Unfortunately, in this instance, things are a little more serious. You're trapped in The Quagmire, a rune indicating that your life is stuck firmly in place. You didn't necessarily do anything to create this goo, but that isn't going to help you when it's oozing in over the tops of your boots.

The thing is, unless you were travelling in a group (and, believe us, that's more information than we need to know about your toilet habits), how are you ever going to get out of this sticky situation? There's only one way to be sure, and that's calling out for help. That's not going to be easy because, let's face it, you're hardly at your best right now, are you? You are – in the most literal sense imaginable – shit out of luck. So, while you wait for the RAC[8] to arrive, why not take the opportunity to look around you? What appears at first glance to be a pit of inhospitable slime is actually a thriving ecosystem. Once you become familiar with some of the less seemly elements that live down here, you may find yourself making some valuable new friends – you know: lawyers, investment bankers, politicians . . .

---

[8] Rescue from Anal Calamities. Call them on 0800-OH-SHIT.

🧻 What Action Can I Take?

As we already mentioned, the best thing you can do when stuck in The Quagmire is to remain still and wait for someone to come along and pull you out. We know that sounds awfully passive but, trust us, struggling only makes it worse. You might think it feels disgusting to have shit leaking over the tops of your boots but it's a walk in the park compared with having it invade your shirt collar. It isn't like quicksand from a Hollywood Western. This stuff doesn't just *brush* off: you can spend weeks picking bits of dried crap out of your pocket.

Historical Context

Bo Weinberg, lieutenant and chief enforcer for the famous gangster Dutch Schultz, is the historical figure most closely associated with The Quagmire. The stories vary, but what is incontrovertible is that Weinberg disappeared in 1935 after Schultz became suspicious of his loyalty, and the smart money is on his being fitted with a pair of concrete overshoes. And you can't get much more 'stuck' than that, can you?

As with those who pass The Quagmire, Weinberg was caught, unable to help himself. His only option, the one outlined above, was to call for somebody else's help – but did he? Well, yeah. Obviously. Cried like a baby. Well, wouldn't you? The point is . . . what is the point? Yeah! The point is: just ask for help, all right? There's no other way out.

Inverted

The Quagmire is a difficult rune to invert –
unless you're sitting backwards on the toilet,
for some bizarre reason. Practising your horse
riding while you back one out? Too much LSD and you think
you're on your motorbike? Who knows. The salient point is
that, no matter how it got there (you freak), it's every bit
as inexplicable upside down as it is the right way up. Squint
and you can almost see the trapped figure calling for help
in The Quagmire. But turn that upside down and you've got
a figure upside down in midair, flying through the air with
the greatest of ease. Yup, it's the Trapeze Artist – a graceful
figure free from the earthly confines down below. While it's
exciting to fly around up there, it's worth bearing in mind
that safety nets *do* fail from time to time and, no matter
how good you are on the trapeze, you still need someone to
catch you.

The Bat

Quick Reading

You may think you're seeing the world clearly, but things aren't always what they seem. Perhaps it's time you started trusting your other senses.

Rites of Passage

Calm & Serene

A whole new way of life can be yours if you will just forego your overreliance on how things look, open up your full range of senses, and enjoy the freedom to hear, touch and taste the world. Perhaps not smell, though. Not just at the moment.

Sound & Fury

There is an old proverb in the Arsetrology business: 'When you live life upside down, it's not just the blood that rushes to your head.'

What Did You Eat?

It's difficult to speculate as to what could have produced such a weirdly-shaped stool, but we're experts at this, so we'll hazard a couple of guesses. Uh . . . a coat hanger . . . and . . . um . . . a dog's bone? That's about all we can come up with, because that's one odd-shaped turd. Speaking slightly more realistically for a moment, bats produce guano, which is a prized fertiliser rich in ammonia, phosphorous and nitrogen, none of which are things you're likely to have ingested unless you look at that box of cleaning products under the sink as your own private cocktail cabinet.

 **Detailed Reading**

Short of breath? Pain behind the eyes? Feeling a little dizzy? No, it's not just the result of the intestinal gymnastics required to pass this particular stool, but the effects of the rune itself. The manifestation of The Bat means that you've been hanging upside down for too long. This has led to all manner of problems, not least of which is the fact that you've been looking at everything the wrong way round. And your nice new hat is lying on the ground beneath you, filled with poo.

Look at it this way: we receive and process information in a number of ways, and in many respects sight is the least reliable. For example, how many times have you been out on the lash with the boys and managed to pull a young lady you are *certain* is the girl of your dreams, only to wake up trapped under a nightmare of morning breath and whale blubber, and having to chew your own arm off so as to escape without waking the beast? That's because you believed what your eyes told you, and eyes can be fooled by a sufficient application of strong lager. Now, if you'd listened to your ears, you'd have heard your mates laughing and peppering their conversation with terms such as 'moose' (despite your not being in rural Canada), 'beer goggles', 'how could you?' and – and this should really have been a giveaway – 'not even with *yours*, mate'.

What Action Can I Take?

What, indeed? Stop eating coat hangers and dogs' bones, for a start. You can also start trusting your hearing, smell, taste and touch. Listen to the music, smell the coffee, taste the difference, reach out and touch someone. Then ask yourself whether you always talk in advertising slogans, or whether it's a temporary side effect of The Bat (all the blood rushing to your head, you see). That's it, really. Make sure you're using all of your senses to collect information about the world and you won't go too far wrong.

The secret of *The Bat* is that your future is what you make it. Let go of your perch, unleash the full range of perception and spread your wings. Oh, and fly. Because, if you don't, you're going to impact the ground at an acceleration of 10 metres per second squared and break every bone in your body. And nobody wants that.

Historical Context

Obviously, the most appropriate historical figure for this rune is Batman.[9] Tragic as his origin was, young Bruce Wayne used all of his senses to cope with the terrible tragedy that left him orphaned. He *saw* the cowardly thug who shot and killed his parents in front of his eyes. He *heard* the roar of the pistol that ended their lives. He *smelled* the gunpowder that propelled the fatal bullets that changed his world for ever. He *tasted* the need for vengeance and righteousness that gave birth to a legend. And he reached out and *touched* the criminals of Gotham City – very hard and very often.

---

[9] He is so too real!

The Bat

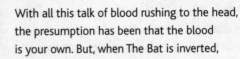

Inverted

With all this talk of blood rushing to the head, the presumption has been that the blood is your own. But, when The Bat is inverted, it's transformed into a far more predatory rune – that of The Vampire. While most people presume that he's a myth, anyone who's spoken to their bank manager lately knows that the parasitic bloodsucker is alive and well. The appearance of the rune in your toilet bowl indicates that you're getting that bloodlust and you're in the mood to pounce. Whether your intended target is a fatted calf, a comely maiden or just an extra-rare steak, your thirst must be slaked.

The Bat

The Hedgehog

Quick Reading

Beneath a prickly exterior lurks one of life's most endearing – but least resilient – creatures.

 ## Rites of Passage

Calm & Serene

OK, you're cute, and everyone knows you are. Sure, there's the occasional attempt on your life while you're crossing the road – but isn't it worth putting up with the odd prick for that much love?

Sound & Fury

You know that 'light at the end of the tunnel' that people talk about? Truck.

What Did You Eat?

Excellent question. A doughnut with Twiglets stuck in it? A Lincolnshire sausage and half a dozen French fries? An actual hedgehog? The possibilities are almost endless, and that's appropriate, since the hedgehog is a fairly omnivorous eater. True, he prefers insects to most other foodstuffs, so you might think about whether you swallowed any bugs last time you took a bike ride.

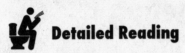 **Detailed Reading**

Whether it's squashed by traffic, burned in a bonfire or just dying from an infestation of parasites, the hedgehog is a pretty hapless animal. Needless to say, the appearance of one in your toilet bowl doesn't bode well. Still, it's not all doom and gloom, is it? Don't be ridiculous – of course, it is. Haven't you been paying attention?

This is a rune that, unlike its namesake, has no upside. Either you're going to suffer yourself or your prickly problem is going to puncture somebody else's happiness. As with a sports car on a country lane, there's no predicting where the next problem is going to come from, and this could well make you nervous and flighty. Try to remain calm, though – panicking is just going to make you run into the road without thinking. And we all know where that leads.

Furthermore, it's no use relying on your inbuilt defence mechanism. Curling into a ball and presenting your spikes to potential enemies may have worked once, but predators these days come with sixteen wheels, air brakes and a marked reluctance to slow down for small mammals. Perhaps you'd be better off hiding in a hedge for a little while longer.

What Action Can I Take?

The secret here is to identify the nature of the problem and to devise a solution that fits that problem. If you translate the rune as meaning that trouble is headed your way, then you need to take evasive action while you come up with a plan to deal with it. Step out of the danger zone, study your foe and repel it carefully and cleverly.

If you decide that The Hedgehog denotes a situation where your prickly exterior has caused some pain to a loved one,[10] then you need to work out what you're doing that's hurting them, and stop it. Either that or buy yourself a leather gimp outfit, swap your oversensitive loved one for a down-to-earth self-harmer, and get down to some good, old-fashioned corporal punishment. And the next time you hear the words 'That hurt, you prick!' you can be sure they'll be said with love.

 Historical Context

Harsh, prickly exterior covering up a soft, cuddly centre? Who else can it be but gang-busting, commie-hunting, cross-dressing FBI director J. Edgar Hoover. Records of Hoover's bowel movements are, of course, classified,[11] so we can only speculate as to whether or not he ever actually passed a hedgehog (there is some speculation about gerbils, but that's not really relevant to our discussion). What is common knowledge is that, like a hedgehog in a bad mood, he rubbed everyone up the wrong way.

With an uncompromising attitude to law enforcement,

---

[10] Oh, all right, then. How do hedgehogs make love? Very carefully! There. Happy now?

[11] 'Plop Secret'. Obviously.

J. Edgar Hoover was a thorn in the side of organised crime –
bank robbers, communists, Mafiosi, spies, moonshiners and
kidnappers all had cause to feel they'd been spiked by the
FBI's first director. But there were hints of a more mellow
side hidden beneath the briery. Although less likely to curl up
into a ball as he was to apply a red-hot curling iron *to* your
balls, Hoover nevertheless did have a soft spot hidden inside
– namely a rather fetching silk camisole. And, now that we've
told you that, we're afraid we're going to have to kill you.

Inverted

The Hedgehog, for all the unrelenting
negativity of the rune, is surprisingly easy
to read when inverted. Upside down, it is,
quite obviously, a jellyfish. The relationship between the
two alignments is unmistakable – one may be hard and
prickly, the other soft and squashy, but they have one trait in
common: hedgehog or jellyfish, it doesn't half sting your ring
piece on the way out.

The good news is that the inverted rune is every bit as
positive as the upright rune is negative. So, if you've plopped
out an upside-down hedgehog, rejoice, for all will be well.
You will float in the gentle ocean of life, looking beautiful
and graceful – but nobody in their right mind will fuck with
you for fear of being stung to within an inch of their life.
Sweet.

The Kraken

Quick Reading

You've unwittingly created a monster and it's too late to get the beast back in the cage.

 Rites of Passage

Calm & Serene

Congratulations! The blue whale is now only the *second*-biggest thing in the ocean. This is a momentous sign and, as long as you haven't prolapsed while passing this beast, you should be ready to reap your reward.

Sound & Fury

Does the world suddenly seem less sure than it was? Do you feel as if things are too big for you? Are you suddenly much diminished from your former state? Not surprising, really – you *have* just lost half your body weight . . .

What Did You Eat?

Whatever it was, it's gone now. All of it. Seriously, if we'd passed something that monstrous, we'd be checking for bits of our small intestine in the bowl, 'cause you just *know* something that size isn't going down without a fight. Really, the only effect your diet is going to have on The Kraken is one of positioning.

If you have a protein-heavy diet, high on meat and low on those weird growy things that the hippies insist on eating, your plop is almost certainly going to have a strong fat content, and your Kraken will be floating on the surface – indicating an obvious, but imposing, threat.

The Kraken

If, on the other hand, you're one of those irritating people who have a perfectly balanced diet and make sure they get their prescribed daily allowance of every weird and fucked-up green vegetable on the planet, then you're likely to have less fat in your shit. The result of this, before you adopt the usual holier-than-thou, my-body-is-a-temple bullshit, is that your Kraken will lurk beneath the surface, making it (a) harder to see until it is almost upon you, and (b) more likely to cause indelible skid marks.

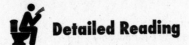 Detailed Reading

Behold! Emerging from the waters like a mighty leviathan comes The Kraken, a fearsome creature that brings destruction wherever it doth travel. Cower in terror! Bow in fear! None are safe from the wrath of this mighty beast! The Kraken must be appeased with an offering! Invest in a new toilet brush[12] or buy some floral air freshener.

Ahem. Examining things a little more calmly, the arrival of The Kraken is indeed momentous, but it doesn't necessarily indicate the end of the world. Instead, this rune is a sign that powerful forces are at work. Perhaps they exist in clear sight – in which case, you are forewarned and may be able to use them to your advantage. Perhaps they lurk unseen, a danger to shipping and a threat to be navigated carefully.

Your mission, should you choose to accept it, is to make use of the powerful forces that have recently surfaced and either avoid their malevolence or use their potency to better your own situation. But be wary: once the monster is awake, it cannot easily be subdued.[13] Think carefully about what you're getting into.

---

[12] No, seriously. You don't honestly think you're going to be able to use the old one after you've pushed *that* fucker down the S-bend, do you?

⟨◍⟩ **What Action Can I Take?**

What, indeed? Traditionally, there have been two very distinct responses to the appearance of a kraken. By far the most common reaction was to run like fuck. Or sail like fuck, if you like. Since we're now in the realm of metaphor rather than life-or-death maritime decisions, perhaps we can afford to be a bit generous with our terminology. In any case, the point to remember here is that a hasty retreat is not the answer. Figuratively, it's not possible to run away from your problems: they'll still be there when you return, and you may even run into new ones during your headlong flight.

We mentioned a second option. The braver, or more foolhardy, souls used to reach for the harpoon when a kraken raised its ugly head. Again, this wasn't clever then, and it's not clever now. Consider the sailor on his ship, gazing into the gaping maw of a monster so huge and hideous that it could wrestle the mighty sperm whale to its death. Drawing its attention to you by flinging a barbed spike at it is hardly a brilliant long-term survival strategy.

Now, consider yourself, faced with The Kraken. You could attempt to harpoon it to death with the toilet brush, but before you do so, we'd urge you to take a moment to consider the full impact of what you're about to do. Go on: picture yourself stabbing again and again at the offending bog, bits of poo bursting off everywhere, turd tentacles creeping up to the rim of the bowl, and befouled water exploding over the floor in a brown tidal wave. Do you think that's likely to solve anything? Or just create more problems?

---

[13] We mean this literally. You may be tempted, after several unsuccessful flushes, to attempt to remove the beast manually. This would be a mistake. You cannot stand against it and win. Large and threatening it may be, but be aware that, even as you scent victory, it could all slip through your fingers like shit through a goose.

35

The Kraken

 **Historical Context**

The early-twentieth-century American horror writer Howard Phillips Lovecraft's entire oeuvre is dominated by terrifying, supernatural things, so impossibly alien that the mere sight of one can flay the sanity from a man's mind. So it should surprise no one to learn that, when Lovecraft conceived his best-known creation, the squamous, betentacled Cthulhu, he had just hopped off the potty and been driven mad by the hideous, rugose shit monster he'd left behind. And if, like us, you've ever stumbled off the bog the morning after, half a bottle of whisky the worse for wear and the beast from forty thousand fathoms writhing in the bowl, trying to pull your bits off with its suckers, then you'll know exactly how he felt.

 Inverted

The inverted Kraken resembles nothing so much as a giant, mutant paw print, which signifies that the menace posed by The Kraken has migrated from sea to land. The significance, of course, being that it has become a solid, quantifiable threat, rather than a lurking, unseen menace.

On the other hand, it could mean that you've disregarded all of our advice above and tried to beat the big, scary shit to death with a toilet brush after all. The inevitable result – *as you were warned* – was a tsunami of poo flowing over the bowl onto your bathroom floor. And now you've got it all over your feet and have trodden it into the carpet throughout the rest of the house.

The Beggar

Quick Reading

You're as hungry as you've ever been – and no wonder! Take a closer look at what's left in the bowl. See that big curly bit at the bottom? That's your lower intestine.

 Rites of Passage

Calm & Serene

There is a certain Zen-like peace in realising that you need to ask for help and being able to do so without losing your pride. Well done. Here: have 10p.

Sound & Fury

'Because I spent all my money on booze' is *not* a reasonable excuse for not eating properly. No sympathy here, we're afraid – you've brought this whole problem on yourself.

What Did You Eat?

Rather a cruel question, really, as the answer is likely to be 'nothing' or 'whatever I found in the dumpster behind KFC'. Let's deal with this in the metaphorical sense (because, if you really are homeless and hungry, we'd suggest that maybe you shouldn't be spending your money on books about poo) and try to convey the point that what you ate may not have been of your choosing. Think carefully – has a friend had you round for dinner lately? At the time you found his protestations that the meal was 'nothing special' to be disarmingly modest; upon mature reflection, however, you realise that your host didn't seem too keen actually to eat any of it himself . . .

 **Detailed Reading**

That growling noise coming from the pit of your stomach is the unmistakable sound of hunger – or possibly the harbinger of a violent bout of diarrhoea, the likes of which will make the eruption of Vesuvius seem like the light froth on the top of a cappuccino. Either way, it can be ignored no longer. There's something missing from your life and, at the moment, it seems that you can't find a way to get it.

This is, of course, entirely unsatisfactory. It's proof positive that the world is a fundamentally unfair place. There's no escaping the anger and frustration born of perceived injustice – and there are few things more unjust than finding yourself in the situation where others have a better job, bigger house, faster car and prettier wife/husband/partner based solely on the fact that they've made something of their lives while you've sat around in your underwear, downloading porn, assigning meaning to the shape of your turds and showing up to work only for payday and leaving drinks.

So, you've got only two options, really, haven't you? Either get up off your arse,[14] pull yourself together and start treating your life and yourself with some respect, or – and how can we put this delicately? – beg. This leads you to implore others for help – an act that does not come naturally to you. Don't be surprised if it leaves a nasty taste in the mouth (eating shit usually does), but get past your initial reluctance and you'll find that people are willing to assist you. Don't abuse this hospitality, however. Just because someone lets you crash on the sofa, it doesn't give you the right to wipe your bum on their cushions.

---

[14] Wipe it first. And wash your hands, for God's sake!

What Action Can I Take?

Essentially, you have two choices: self-improvement and self-pity. People say that when you hit rock bottom, the only way is up – but they've clearly not gone round the bar at four in the morning swigging the remains of everyone else's drink, as we have. (It's not just us, right?)

So: self-improvement. You know the drill, you've heard all the clichés before, we're sure: pull your socks up, get your shit together, grab the bull by the horns and make something of yourself. Interestingly enough, there is one recorded case of a gentleman doing exactly as we suggested. Sadly, it all went horribly wrong, with the net result that he was admitted to A&E with multiple gore wounds, six broken ribs and socks full of shit. It turned out that the only thing he could make of himself was a spectacle.

That leaves us with self-pity, where all the clichés are replaced with questions: *Why me? What did I do to deserve this? Where did it all go wrong? Is that too much to ask?* Unfortunately, the answer to all of these questions is invariably, 'I'm sorry, I think you may have me confused with someone who gives a fuck.' What can we say? Life sucks. Get over it. And remember: there's no shame in asking for help – but whining like a little girl is very unbecoming. Especially when that's coupled with your botty problems.

Historical Context

Difficult one, this. Beggars, by their very nature, tend not to be the sorts of people to write their names indelibly into the history books – although when they do, rather appropriately, necessity inclines them to use shit for ink. Which is nice.

The Beggar

There are, as it happens, a couple of famous beggars, and none more magnificent than Joshua Abraham Norton, the self-proclaimed 'Emperor of the United States'. Born in London and raised in South Africa, Norton arrived in San Francisco in the middle of the nineteenth century, with a small fortune garnered from his father's estate. Although he promptly lost this fortune when his investment in Peruvian rice[15] went tits up.

His Imperial Majesty Emperor Norton I was widely considered to be insane; had he actually had money, that verdict would surely have been revised to 'eccentric'. Possessed of no real political power and respected only so far as he was humoured by those around him, Norton was, in many ways, indistinguishable from every American vice-president except Dick Cheney. Although quite clearly mad, Emperor Norton was treated deferentially in San Francisco. There was even a currency issued in his name, which was honoured in the area he frequented, despite its being barely worth wiping your arse with.

Inverted

The Beggar is one of the more fascinating runes when inverted, with an obvious literal symbolism that should be plain for all to see. There are really only two interpretations that are accepted by FART.[16] The inverted beggar either represents a purse being tipped up and coins falling out – signifying quite clearly that your chosen course of action is not only to beg but that it is guaranteed to be successful – or it's a schematic diagram of your backside opening to release little poo pebbles, thus indicating that you're, ahem, shit out of luck.

---

[15] Which is scientifically proven to make you shit more than normal rice. See how seamlessly it all fits together?

[16] The Federation of Arse Readers and Turdologists.

The Sty

Quick Reading

You've created quite a mess, haven't you? And it's one that you're quite content to wallow in. In fact, you're as happy as a pig in ... well, you know.

 Rites of Passage

Calm & Serene

The popularising of chaos theory was the best thing that ever happened to you. Now you can maintain that it's not mess, but a system too complex to comprehend.

Sound & Fury

You can spout off about chaos theory until the cows come home — the fact of the matter is that you're a disgrace. Shape up or ship out, Pigpen.

What Did You Eat?

Ha! What *didn't* you eat? This isn't the sort of mess that derives from a balanced diet. Take a good look at your shit.[17] Four straight turds in strict alignment, but kept apart by mysterious means. Well, maybe mysterious to medical science, but those of us versed in the noble art of Arsetrology know a repulsive force when we see one. It couldn't be clearer if you were shitting magnets. Each of the major food groups has accreted together to form a separate island of once-food. It's safe to assume that the small one is the stuff that's good for you.

---

[17] You know you want to. Pervert!

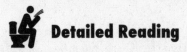

Detailed Reading

That's quite a mess you've created. Glorious, isn't it? You know you should be disgusted with yourself, but there's a part of you (the part that watches *Strictly Come Dancing* in the vain hope that one of the dancers' tits will pop out) that is actually rather proud of all this filth. Others may call you a slob, but the way you see it you're comfortable in your own skin, wherever that is (under all the dirt and scabs, presumably).

Of course, despite the above exhortation to *have a wash, you dirty bastard*, the mess may not be actual but metaphorical: a sticky situation you've got yourself into in your work, home life or relationship. Not that that bothers you – nothing can distract you from the joys of a good wallow. Besides, you know what they say: once you're in the shit, it's only a matter of how deep you sink. The thing is, though, that this filth-encrusted environment is keeping you from progressing. You may think you're soaking up the atmosphere, but take a closer look. That's not atmosphere: it's shit.

What Action Can I Take?

Well, the first thing you can do – and we can't overemphasise the importance of this – is to *stop wallowing in shit*. Jesus Christ, what do you need, a personal invitation? Get. Out. Of. The. Poo. The thing about The Sty is that everybody else can see it for what it is – four walls, a locked gate and a carpet of shite – except you. Even if you're convinced that your filthy hovel is a palace, the feeling that this isn't the way things should be keeps nagging away at you, like an itch you can't scratch. Or maybe that's scabies.

No, the truth is that you're feeling hemmed in by something, and, in a spectacular reversion to the anal-retentive stage, you've decided to make of that restriction a virtue, and revel in your imprisonment. This is no way to live, so look beyond the walls in which you've enclosed yourself, see your problem for what it is and sally forth to defeat it. Just make sure you wipe your feet before you go.

🏛 Historical Context

Just as the perpetrator of The Sty wallows in shite, unable to accept that he's hemmed in and covered in crap, so the last Julio-Claudian emperor of Rome indulged himself while the city burned. Yes, Lucius Domitius Ahenobarbus – better known to the world as Nero – is an archetypal Sty figure. It is a well-known fact[18] that Nero fiddled[19] while Rome burned, and, though having one off the wrist may, on the surface, have little in common with avoiding your problems by taking solace in a cage of crap, to do so while the greatest city in the world goes up in flames around you bears the same basic hallmarks of utterly avoiding the problem in hand.

Inverted

From the ridiculous to the sublime. While The Sty is a humble structure, homely in appearance, simple in construction and smelling – let's face it – of shit, inverted this rune takes on a very different significance. Put simply, it's Stonehenge, isn't

---

[18] And is, therefore, almost certainly false.
[19] Knocking one out can be a powerful method of divination. Wankomancy (as it's known) is generally considered the hairy-handed cousin of Arsetrology.

it? Which is great on the one hand – because who doesn't love Stonehenge? On the other hand . . .

Stonehenge is a mystery in very many ways. From an archaeological viewpoint, no one really knows where it came from or what it's for. From a tourist's viewpoint, it's usually a bit of a disappointment – *Is that it? Oh. It looks bigger on the TV. . .* And, from a hippy's viewpoint, it's a chance to get the leg over some unsuspecting, awestruck undergraduate at one of the solstice rituals. So expect some hairy-legged nookie heading your way sometime soon.

The Metronome

Quick Reading

Everybody knows how important it is to keep regular and at the moment you're not missing a beat. Bored yet?

 Rites of Passage

Calm & Serene

An extremely gratifying rune (so to speak). Everything about your life seems to be running (again: so to speak) as smoothly as clockwork. Don't change a thing!

Sound & Fury

Oh dear! We *are* stuck in a rut, aren't we? You may be fooling yourself into thinking that your life is stable, but, let's face it, it's *dull*. Trust us: nothing says 'life is shit' like dropping The Metronome.

What Did You Eat?

As a metronome's primary purpose is keeping time, its appearance in the toilet bowl suggests that your diet has plenty of ingredients to keep you regular. From where we're standing (namely, at a safe distance) it looks as if you're getting exactly your Recommended Daily Allowance of roughage, which has produced this perfectly formed rune. We're talking bran, wholemeal bread, porridge oats and all sorts of food too bland to mention. Like the Metronome itself, these all have one thing in common – they're all boring as fuck. Would it kill you to go for the chocolate-chip cookies rather than the oatcakes, just for once? Live a little, man!

Detailed Reading

Look, everybody wants a little stability in their life. There's a reason we try to establish a set routine for young children – and it's not *all* about stopping their parents taking a quick trip to the Land of Mental. Routine is good: it allows us to get through the less interesting aspects of day-to-day living without much thought, thereby saving up the grey matter for when things get complex. And, if that's what you're doing, then consider The Metronome to be a vindication of your exemplary life plan. (Just don't expect an invitation round to mine for dinner, you boring, boring bastard.)

If, however, you find yourself living the kind of life where Tuesday night is sausage-and-chips night and you start to feel yourself hyperventilating if you have pie and peas, then you're in desperate need of a change. In which case, The Metronome has come around at just the right time. Listen to your stool (no, not literally) and find some change in your life.

Your desire for order is bordering on obsession and this sort of repetition isn't natural. If it continues much longer, then even the most level-headed individual is liable to crack under the strain. So, unless you want your next trip to the post office to end up as a *News at Ten* item that concludes with a distraught neighbour describing you as 'such a quiet man' and an opinion piece on gun control, we'd consider this a timely reminder to enact some change in your life.

What Action Can I Take?

Well, that very much depends on whether you view the appearance of The Metronome as a sign that you have imposed order on the chaos of life, or as an indication that you're stuck in a rut. If the former, then there's not really any action *to* take, is there? You don't turn the steering wheel if you're on a straight stretch of road. But, if you feel you're a hamster on the wheel of life, it's probably time to effect some changes – taking a different route to work, getting a hobby, quitting your job or having an affair are all valid responses to The Metronome.[20]

Historical Context

It will probably come as no surprise to you to discover that the historical figure most closely identified with The Metronome is Benito Mussolini. After all, it's a well-known feature of fascist states that routine is king. Recently discovered journals kept by Il Duce's personal physician describe regular passing of a peculiarly shaped stool that we now recognise as The Metronome. *Say what you want about Mussolini*, goes the aphorism, *but at least he got the trains to run on time.* And now we know how.

---

[20] And the lawsuits start flooding in. – Ed.

Inverted

While undoubtedly similar in form when inverted, this rune – while sharing essential elements with The Metronome – differs in its fundamental function. Sure, it maintains a steady rhythm and tick-tocks back and forth, but this is for something more than simple timekeeping. This is The Windscreen Wiper, sweeping back and forth across your viewport and ensuring you have a clear view on the world. While it's not the most exciting piece of equipment on a car – oiks from Romford don't bother customising their wipers when they can add another neon strip or subwoofer to their ludicrously overpumped Escort – it does serve a purpose.

But, while road-safety experts are keen on the wiper, the Arsetrologist knows that it makes it difficult to effect any lasting change on the surface. The Metronome may be an impetus for change, but The Windscreen Wiper makes it nigh on impossible. However, only a fool would switch them off when it's raining.

The Hullabaloo

Quick Reading

You're all set to create a stink – but who benefits from this mess?

 Rites of Passage

Calm & Serene

At last, people are starting to sit up and take notice of you – and this time it's not because you shat yourself at the office Christmas party.

Sound & Fury

Pay attention to me! Pay attention to me! Everyone pay attention to me! This is celebrity-culture narcissism at its worst – you'll do anything for attention, even create chaos in the lives of those around you.

What Did You Eat?

At the risk of indulging in bad poetry: The Hullabaloo is all about you. So, you've probably eaten whatever you damn well please – and, unless you're an irredeemable vegan weirdo, that means loads of high-sugar, high-carb, low-nutrition, takeaway rubbish. Still, no matter what you're stuffing in your gob, *nothing* explains the reeking blob of cartoon-speech-balloon-shaped wrongness currently infesting your toilet bowl.

No, the appearance of The Hullabaloo must be taken seriously as an indicator of change. That change can be positive or negative. Either your manifold talents are about to be recognised by a hitherto ignorant world or you're

49

about to go postal in an over-the-top, take-no-prisoners, no-holds-barred attempt to shock an uncaring world into finally acknowledging your natural place among the elite.

Detailed Reading

If The Hullabaloo signifies a positive outcome, there's really very little you need to do — accept the plaudits graciously, don't let your head swell up with all the compliments and try to behave in the sort of dignified manner that's so patently absent in 95 per cent of Premier League footballers. If, however, the writing in the speech balloon says something different — such as 'Hey! How about you arseholes listen to *me* for a change?' — then we have some work to do.

If you get caught on the wrong end of The Hullabaloo, you may find yourself huffing and puffing about the smallest details, getting upset over nothing, ready to blow your stack at a moment's notice. It's not that things are any worse than usual, but rather that your levels of tolerance have dropped considerably. Trivialities take on an inflated importance, while the really important things drift out to the sidelines, like a turd in a swimming pool.

Your outrage may take many forms. You may find yourself compelled to write indignant letters to the newspapers, stage a sit-in[21] protest, or even take to the streets with a placard in order to express your fury at something that's doubtless none of your business. These are all perfectly legal and acceptable forms of making clear your displeasure. Free expression is a wonderful thing, but always bear in mind that the influence of The Hullabaloo is less about the issue at hand and more about your desperate need for attention.

---

[21] Surely you can insert the 'h' yourself? Believe it or not, we do have *some* decorum left.

What Action Can I Take?

However it manifests itself, your inability to keep your opinions to yourself can have some dangerous consequences. Righteous indignation is rarely an attractive quality and people around you will quickly tire of your inflated opinions – not to mention the disturbing squelching sounds of your prolapsed anus flapping in the breeze. Some will simply turn their backs and ignore you. Others, however, will rise to your challenge and could well leave you with a bloody nose to go with your ruined backside.

How to address the issue? Well, first we'd recommend fixing the obvious physical damage. Push what's left of your ring piece back up your bum, pack the wound with something soft and absorbent, such as cotton balls, and repair the breach with superglue or a similar adhesive.[22]

Next, bring yourself back down to earth. We'd recommend a short, sharp dose of perspective. When your ego is getting more out of control than a C-list celebrity in the jungle, simply consider the fact that you're choosing to spend your time examining your own shit and believe that this somehow has some kind of significance.

Not so bloody self-important now, are you?

Historical Context

A slight departure, this time: cultural rather than historical context. And the winner is . . . everyone who's ever been a housemate on *Big Brother*. What better reflects the desperate need for attention and fame than this grotesque

---

[22] Are you kidding me? Who checked this manuscript for legal liability? We could be sued into the poorhouse over this sort of shit – and if I go down, I'm taking you two with me. – Ed.

The Hullabaloo

parade of increasingly ill-tempered, ill-mannered, ignorant blights on society? All the ills of modern life are present and accounted for. Sexism? Check. Racism? Check. Complete self-absorption? Check. Inability to use polysyllables? Check. Weird speech-balloon-shaped shit stagnating in the toilet bowl? Oh, yes.

Perhaps even worse (or better, depending on whether you're considering how well they fit the Rune or their worth as human beings) is the sociological freak show of *Celebrity Big Brother*. You will not see a sadder collection of attention-seeking has-beens and never-wases. Until the next series. For these people, The Hullabaloo isn't just an Arsetrological rune: it's a physical manifestation of their talent. It's a reeking, corn-filled reminder of just how low we've allowed the celebrity bar to be lowered.

Inverted

Where The Hullabaloo is all about an explosion of bluster, it's inverted form is a lot more subdued. It's still an exhortation, but it's spoken downwards, as if its speaker were mumbling into their chest. And it's a shame, because, where The Hullabaloo is all loud, arrogant bullshit, The Murmur is actually the best idea no one ever got to hear. You might find yourself lacking the confidence to speak up when under the influence of The Murmur and your ideas could well be ignored by those around you. It's not that they're bad, just that you're not projecting them properly and, if you don't speak up, the only person who's going to hear is Ian from Accounts, who'll wait three days and then claim it as his idea. Don't give him the opportunity – speak up for yourself!

The Dog

Quick Reading

They say familiarity can breed contempt, but that doesn't mean you should rub your old friend's nose in it.

 Rites of Passage

Calm & Serene

Old friends, set routines, familiar ground – these can be signs that you're stuck in a rut but don't discount the possibility that you've simply got everything right. After all, if it ain't broke, don't fix it.

Sound & Fury

Old friends, set routines, familiar ground – doesn't *anything* fucking change? Looks like you're treading water and, unlike with The Metronome, you're determined to do something about it. You can always blame the dog for your farts, but where do you lay the blame for that bizarre crap in the bowl?

What Did You Eat?

Q. What's invisible and smells of dog food?

A. Pensioners' farts. Thank you, thank you . . . We're here all week . . .

All right, so it's a cheap joke, but the point of that riddle was to illustrate how sometimes the food we eat can have a more direct bearing on the runes we produce than any mystic Arsetrological interpretation.

If you're happy with your life – and there must be *somebody* who is – then there's no need to react to The Dog with anything other than a few sheets of toilet paper and a contented smile. If, however, you're feeling a crushing sense of sameness and need to address that, then be careful – ditching your old friends for new can lead to resentment. Remember, there are two types of vengeful dog: the one that bites you right away and then gets on with things; and the one that seems willing to put up with no end of insults without taking offence. Beware this second type – it's just waiting for the best opportunity to take a shit in your slippers.

 ## Detailed Reading

Man's best friend – faithful, loyal and ever present. Alternatively, you could argue that he's stupid, smelly and really needs to do something about that leg-humping thing. You're tending more towards the latter at the moment and you have a real temptation to boot the pooch. Try to resist that urge, as The Dog can be a very useful rune: correctly interpreted, it can strengthen the bonds of loyalty between old friends, provide unconditional support in trying times and fetch the newspaper from the front garden when you're too lazy to go outside.

Abuse The Dog, though, and it will piss on your carpet, steal your dinner from the worktop, leave a crap on the front doormat and be off before you can say, 'Wait a moment, we don't *have* a dog.' Even the best of friends can be pushed only so far before he bites back.

What Action Can I Take?

Regular exercise and a balanced diet are essential for keeping your dog healthy and happy. But who gives a shit about that? We're talking metaphors, here. So: it never hurts to help shore up old friendships with an offering. Throw them a bone or two, go for a walk with them, offer up compliments – for example 'Hi, Bill, you're looking well. May I say how wet and shiny your nose is looking today? Mind if I have a quick sniff of your arse to see how things are down there?' What true friend could say no?

On the other hand, dogs get worms, ticks and fleas, so you need to be well protected against infestations. This – again – is a metaphor and as such open to liberal interpretation, but essentially means you should exercise caution in your dealings. Don't just throw away years of happiness on the promise of something new. They say you can't teach an old dog new tricks – but, if the *old* trick is to go outside when he wants a crap, it's worth its weight in carpet cleaner.

Historical Context

Faithful. Loyal. Ever present. Willing to chase whatever stick you happen to throw him. Humps your leg when feeling amorous. It's Doctor Watson, isn't it? Think about it. He was Sherlock Holmes's constant companion (man's best friend); he did all the heavy lifting and drudge work while Holmes stood around enjoying the polite conversation of society's elite ('Fetch my slippers while I sit back and sup this port'); he covered for Holmes when the detective was lost in the embrace of the opium ('What's that terrible smell?' 'Oh, the dog's farted again! Bad dog! Bad!'); and, most of all, he provided an uncritical admiration of Holmes's vast

55

intellect (Watson didn't *quite* bound up to the door panting whenever Sherlock came home. But he might as well have).

Inverted

Turning this rune upside down doesn't produce an immediately clear image in one's mind, so, to understand the nature of inversion, we're going off the page a little bit. It's occurred to many a stoned student that 'God' is 'Dog' spelled backwards, but very few have ever been able to gain any insight into what this means. Well, here comes Arsetrology to the rescue, because in this context God is a perfect inversion of The Dog.

Where the dog craves affection, God demands respect. Where the dog is subservient, God is a thundering, all-powerful despot. And, where the Dog bites postmen, God shoves a lightning bolt up their arse. OK, so the existence of God is a contentious issue, whereas no one disputes the existence of Dog, but, if you want to avoid being struck down by the Almighty, you might want to get down on your knees, pray and love thy log.

The Banker

Quick Reading

Flushed with success? Or crushed by expectations? This is certainly all about money, but which way is it flowing – down the S-bend or up over the bowl?

∿ Rites of Passage

Calm & Serene

Looks like fortune favours the brave – and who is braver than the man who can look upon the structural impossibility of The Banker and not feel overwhelmed by the symbolism?[23]

Sound & Fury

Well, isn't that just fucking great? The disconnection warnings and the overdraft that looks like a phone number were clues enough that you're in a spot of financial bother – you didn't actually need supernatural dollar signs forming out of shit in the one place you have a right to expect some peace.

🍔 What Did You Eat?

Whatever it was, we hope it wasn't expensive. Your days of Dom Perignon and lobster thermidor are over, my friend. And the only way you'll be seeing *foie gras* any time soon is if your own liver explodes under the relentless pressure of that job lot of cheap supermarket-brand lager you've spent your last pennies on. Even then, you'll need to change your pants to see it.

---

[23] And the smell. Never forget the smell.

 **Detailed Reading**

We've made a lot of symbolism in this book and usually for very good reason – in any form of fortune-telling, there are layers of unreality and illusion to be stripped away before you get your first glimpse at the truth. Occasionally, though, there comes a rune that cuts through the mystical mumbo-jumbo and gets right to the point. There are no metaphors at work here. It is a literal, rather than a symbolic, truth that bankers belong in the toilet – with all the other shit.

You may *think* they're all right when your investment portfolio overfloweth and you're raking in money hand over fist, but all they *really* see while they're offering you an investment opportunity is a shortcut to making their indoor swimming pool one degree warmer in winter. Put simply, there's a reason the collective noun for bankers is a 'wunch'.

That's all a bit doom-'n'-gloom, you might think; what about the upside? It's true that, like any Arsetrological rune, The Banker can go either way, but let's face it: you wouldn't be putting your trust in the mystic power of shite if everything was coming up roses and dividends, now, would you? No, no – you're fucked and we won't insult you by pretending you're not. The best way forward now is to see if we can minimise the damage.

What Action Can I Take?

How should we know? Seriously, if we knew enough to drag you out of the financial mess you've got yourself into and advise a strategy for fiscal security, do you really think we'd be probing and interpreting people's crap for a living? This isn't a get-rich-quick book, so all we can suggest is the obvious. Get a better job. Stop blowing your money on cheap booze and hookers. Rob a bank.[24] Sell a kidney. Do whatever it is that people who don't spend all day coming up with poo jokes do in order to make ends meet. And, in the meantime, could you lend us twenty quid?

Historical Context

If we're talking bankers, we must be talking the Rothschilds. However, with the attention to detail and pants-wetting fear of the author who has no desire to be sued into a smoking crater by a financial juggernaut like the Rothschild family, we would like to state for the record that Nathan Mayer Rothschild was absolutely *not* a grasping capitalist monster with more respect for money than for human life. Probably.

But he *was* a banker – and a pretty bloody impressive one, we must say. A founder of the mighty Rothschild banking dynasty, lender of money to the Bank of England, textile merchant, mining magnate, sexual dynamo[25] and world champion sudoku player,[26] Nathan Rothschild almost certainly shat gold ingots,[27] so who are we to mock him?

---

[24] Getting really sick of the 'please sue us' phrases. Is *nobody* checking this manuscript for legal ramifications? – Ed.

[25] You can't prove this, can you? – Ed.

[26] Or this? – Ed.

[27] Now you're just being silly. – Ed.

Inverted

What do you get when you turn money upside down? Upside-down money, clearly. Sorry, but if you've dropped this most unlikely of all poos into your porcelain, it doesn't matter which way up it is: you are dirt poor and the only pleasure you have left has just reminded you of that sorry fact.

The Mineshaft

Quick Reading

You're lost in the bowels of the earth, but keep moving – you'll eventually emerge into the light.

 ## Rites of Passage

Calm & Serene

Remain calm. This is a definite vindication of your straight-and-narrow lifestyle.

Sound & Fury

Tread carefully – there's a reason this mine has been abandoned. The slightest noise could start a collapse, so squeeze those bum cheeks together and don't make a sound.

What Did You Eat?

Cornish pasties were invented so that miners could have a decent lunch without poisoning themselves. Covered head to toe in coal dust, they would hold the pasty by the edges and nosh up to the crust, disposing of the dirty remainder by dropping it down the mineshaft as an offering to subterranean sprites known as Knockers.[28] While miners are few and far between these days, the pasty lives on, most often eaten cold from the chiller cabinet of a petrol-station minimart. Perhaps you want to think about laying off the convenience foods and eating a proper meal once in a while.

---

[28] Insert your own innuendo here.

 **Detailed Reading**

You're deep underground and lost in the dank, dark caves. Claustrophobia is setting in and, although the air is musty, you need to take a few deep breaths in order to get your head together – this really is not the time to panic. (Actually, it's not the time to be taking deep breaths, either).

If you're in the habit of keeping a canary in your toilet,[29] it might be an idea to take a peek in its cage about now. If you discover it merrily chirping away as if it hasn't a worry in the world, then all is probably well. If, on the other hand, you find it flat on its back with its little claws pointing skywards, we'd suggest you finish up the paperwork and vacate the fallout zone post-haste.

And, if the worst has happened, how does one cope with confusion that comes with a shaft collapse?[30] We advise patience. It always takes a while for your eyes to adjust to the dark, so don't get ahead of yourself, and allow yourself to get used to the gloom. It's certainly not a good idea to rush anywhere, as falling and injuring yourself means you could be down here longer than you'd like. And you *know* you're going to land in shit, don't you? It's just that sort of a book.

---

[29] What? *Some* people do. We read it in a book.
[30] Have you any idea of the sort of self-control it takes not to make a knob joke, here?

What Action Can I Take?

Mining is hard, dangerous work – but there are well-developed procedures for coping with the peril. Tug on your helmet, get a grip on your axe handle, decide which vein you're going after, and repeat to yourself, 'I am the master of the shaft. *I* am the master of the shaft. I am the master of the *shaaaaaaft*!'[31]

Historical Context

So, this rune leaves us with a bit of a dilemma. The obvious historical personage to associate with The Mineshaft is Arthur Scargill, but he's still alive and, thus, able to litigate our arses off.

Rather than try to pick one miner, we thought we'd refer to thousands of them – namely, the miners who flocked to California during the Gold Rush. Multitudes of dirt-poor Chinese and Latin Americans headed out West to grub out a better life for themselves and their families. Working heroically under adverse conditions, many found their lives were even worse than before. Hmm. Not exactly inspiring, is it? And it doesn't solve our initial problem. Why bother with libel when you can racially abuse the underprivileged? Truth be told, there's just no way to make mining funny.

---

[31] Clearly more self-control than *we* possess . . .

Inverted

Well, it's exactly the same upside down as it is the right way up, and that reflects the hopelessness of your situation. You've been underground for so long that you've lost all sense of direction and don't even know which way is up. It doesn't matter how hard you bang at it with a pickaxe, the walls of The Mineshaft won't budge. Best get comfy and watch out for Knockers.

The Hunter

Quick Reading

There's a trail of spoor to follow – but who is hunting whom? And, more importantly, can you clean it up before anyone else sees it?

 Rites of Passage

Calm & Serene

Ah! The thrill of the chase! Open your senses to the natural world and let yourself become one with nature. After all, if it looks like deer shit, feels like deer shit and tastes like deer shit, it probably *is* deer shit. Good thing you didn't step in it.

Sound & Fury

Face it, there's nothing natural about this hunt, is there? Nothing noble. It's pure mean-spirited revenge. Whaddayamean 'Why do I want to kill it?' I went on a safari and that bloody elephant shat all over me! It took me two weeks to dig my fucking car out . . .

What Did You Eat?

What indeed? And who could tell, for the cunning Hunter can disguise his trail, leaving little clue to his passing. And the master Hunter is so at one with his environment that he can actually lay down a false trail to confuse his enemies. Of course, it could just be a doughnut and a few cocktail sausages, couldn't it?

Detailed Reading

Picking through poo isn't everyone's idea of a good time,[32] but to The Hunter it's an essential tool for tracking down prey. The fact that you're sifting through spoors shows you have the basic method of enquiry. Or that you're a colossal pervert who should be locked up for your own good and the safety of all around you. Could go either way, quite frankly.

The main lesson, though, is that things aren't always what they appear – and this is doubly true when you're tracking down a dangerous foe. Observation is the watchword here, and it's imperative you pay attention to every crack, smear and scent in your immediate environment. Complacency could lead to a swift mauling. Or to finding that you haven't wiped properly and every seat in the house is covered in . . . clues.

Remember: even the most experienced tracker follows false leads now and again, so don't be embarrassed about doubling back on yourself. It pays to be careful and remember that the hunter can very easily become the hunted.

 What Action Can I Take?

What action do you *want* to take? If you consider yourself to be an alpha male (and bear in mind you *are* reading a book about that area where poo and fortune-telling meet) do you really need to do anything? Surely the world reorders itself to your will at the merest whiff of your testosterone. You are The Hunter – go hunt something and stop whining.

---

[32] Although Gillian McKeith certainly seems to enjoy her work.

But, if you're one of life's losers, if the pack leader makes you (and you alone) drink *down*river from the latrine site, then perhaps it's best to interpret this rune as a call to action. Either *follow* the track to a new, more assertive you, or *make* tracks – to a place where your first decision every day isn't whether to hand over your lunch money or have your head flushed down the toilet.

 Historical Context

Who but that American folk hero and legendary hunter, Daniel Boone, could be judged fit for this rune?[33] The stories surrounding Boone are many; some are unverifiable, most are unfeasible and all are filled with the sort of mythic grandeur that surrounds so many Wild West characters.

What we *do* know is that Boone's stamping ground was the area of the United States now known as Kentucky, home of good, strong bourbon whiskey and a particularly delicious, if heart-attack-inducing, method of preparing dead chickens. Destined for fame at a young age, he was, it is said, given his first rifle at the age of twelve, and quickly learned superior hunting skills from the local Indian population.

Legend has it that he and some young friends were out in the woods when they were surprised by a panther. According to the story, while his friends panicked and ran away, Boone calmly took aim and killed the panther with his squirrel gun. If that ain't alpha male Hunter right there, we'll eat our pith helmets.

---

[33] Indeed, who would want to be?

Inverted

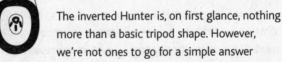

The inverted Hunter is, on first glance, nothing more than a basic tripod shape. However, we're not ones to go for a simple answer when a stupid and/or funny one will do instead, so we're going to say that this is no ordinary tripod. If we said to you that the chances of anything coming from Mars were a million to one, what would be your response? Yup, this innocent looking, three-legged beast is, in fact, a Martian invader from *The War of the Worlds*.

What does this have to do with Arsetrology you ask? Well, you may generally be a bipedal organism, but when you're laying down a pipe you are essentially tripodic[34] and therefore have much in common with our new Martian overlords. You're unintelligible, capable of immense destructive power and generally hell bent on causing as much mess as possible. Where The Hunter sneaks through the undergrowth in search of his prey, you just burn the fucker out with a death ray. Not subtle, but effective.

---

[34] You're not allowed just to make up words, you know. – Ed.

The Lumberjack

Quick Reading

Tim-berrrrr! Others need to be made aware of your mighty logging skills. Shout it to the treetops!

 Rites of Passage

Calm & Serene

You know that old saw, 'The bigger they are, the harder they fall'? Pah! You laugh at such foolishness, for these mighty logs drop from your backside as easy as overripe apples from a tree!

Sound & Fury

Fall, damn you! Fall! This puts an entirely different slant on things. It might . . . be easier . . . to pass . . . the actual . . . tree. Fall! *Argh!*

What Did You Eat?

It's quite an extraordinary feat of anal engineering you've achieved here. It's possible that you've passed Daddy Sausage and Baby Sausage and Mummy Sausage is still on her way through the small intestine, but we have to question how you're producing such straight-and-true turds. Have you been swallowing pencils again? You do know you're supposed to take the corn *off* the cob before you eat it, don't you?

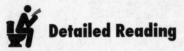 **Detailed Reading**

If a poo falls in a forest, and there's nobody there to hear it, does it still make a smell?

The Lumberjack may seem like a cheap excuse for some obvious log gags, but what it actually illustrates is the importance of picking up new practical skills. It's time to get in touch with the outdoors. Nobody knows the splendour of nature better than the man sent to destroy it, so The Lumberjack is your call to arms. It's time to turn your back on the mollycoddling modern world, with all its digital convenience and airy-fairy ways, and relearn the skills that are your essential manly tools: cutting, sawing, whittling, burning and generally beating the fuck out of whatever comes to hand.

This doesn't necessarily mean you have to engage in a major deforestation campaign – a little bit of woodwork or weed-killing could do the trick. What's important is that you stamp your mark upon Mother Nature and let her know who's boss.

What Action Can I Take?

This is a clear message that you've become too reliant on technology and need to get back to nature. Put away your fussy gadgets and put your own natural implements – namely your horny hands and hampered elbows[35] – to good use by engaging with some essential masculine activities. 'Fair enough,' you say, 'but how?' Good point. It used to be that fathers would teach these skills to their sons, but it seems

---

[35] Although this may look like cheap innuendo, we're actually referring to Whiting Williams's classic 1922 treatise on the European working class. The fact that it sounds a little bit like a wank gag is entirely coincidental. Sometimes you just get lucky.

those days are gone. Both of our fathers work in accounts – the only hunting they do is for fiscally irresponsible departments that exceed their operational budgets.

Luckily, these days, picking up new skills is as easy as falling off a log. All you need to do is decide what manly, physically taxing skill you want to learn and look it up on the Internet. Amazing thing, the Internet – pretty much anything you need to know can be found in its sites and bytes. Hmm. Actually, maybe this technology stuff isn't *all* bad, after all . . .

 Historical Context

To be considered the historical avatar of The Lumberjack, a character would have to be a real man's man, larger than life, possessed of extraordinary physical attributes and with a track record of performing childhood tasks that would be beyond even the most robust of modern men.

He would have to have been so magnificent that, for instance, it took three storks to carry him to his parents as an infant. He would have to have been so strong that, when he laughed for the first time, the vibrations broke every window in his house. He would have to have been so precocious that before he could even walk he sawed the legs off of his parents' bed in the middle of the night. And the stories around him would have to be so ridiculous that one of them claims he dug the Grand Canyon by dragging his axe behind him when he walked.

American readers will already have guessed who we're talking about, but let the rest of you now learn that the historical figure who best suits the rune of The Lumberjack is that mighty man of folklore, that tree-felling giant, that mighty Big Man whose shit, should it fall on you, would crush you without hope of survival: Paul Bunyan.

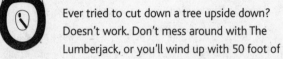

Inverted

Ever tried to cut down a tree upside down? Doesn't work. Don't mess around with The Lumberjack, or you'll wind up with 50 foot of Canadian redwood falling on you. That said, there's a certain song that suggests lumberjacks aren't quite as butch as they try to make out. We're not saying there's any truth to it, but, when you look at an Inverted Lumberjack, you'd be forced to concede that it goes the other way. That's all we're saying.

rtlehead

ding

oke your head out and sniff the air
. Is it safe to emerge? Or should you
o your shell and resume your emotional
ion?

Rites of Passage

n & Serene

ur tough and hardy exterior is the perfect shield, allowing
ou to meet the cold, cruel world head-on, while protecting
your innocence and childlike inability to keep from laughing
whenever anybody says the word 'bum'.

Sound & Fury

Slow and steady wins the race. Yeah, right. If the race is to
see who can die of boredom first. Get a move on, you lazy
bastard, some of us have places to be!

What Did You Eat?

The hard shell contains a soft centre. This is true of both
expensive chocolate selections and dog poo in winter. We
hope it doesn't take any great philosophical insight to realise
that, if you have a choice between eating one of the above,
you'll be better served going for the one that comes wrapped
in coloured foil. As for what else you might have eaten,
the evidence strongly suggests the influence of an unwise
amount of alcohol (see 'What Action Can I Take?' below).

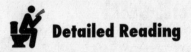 **Detailed Reading**

This is another rune that's all about getting out of your comfort zone. Yes, things have been safe and secure for a while now, but, while you've been straining to keep hold of things, you've only ended up postponing the inevitable. We're sure you've heard the warning signs and felt the tremors, but you've ignored the indicators for so long that you can't hold back any longer.

When The Turtlehead pops out, things really have reached zero hour. You've contained yourself until the last possible moment and it may well be too late to do anything about it. Still, the fact that you're finally acknowledging the problem is a step in the right direction,[36] albeit a slow and faltering one. The question, now, is whether the turtle can pull its head back inside its body, or whether the extension can continue further and remain out in the open for all to see.

 What Action Can I Take?

Given that 'action' is about as far removed from The Turtlehead as 'good taste' is from this entire book, this is a difficult one to answer. It may be that your hard, protective shell is the perfect way to interact with an imperfect world, while still keeping a part of yourself unsullied by modern life.

However, if you fear that the crusty hard exterior of The Turtlehead is keeping you from your destiny (and you could do worse, in this instance, than consider 'destiny' a polite way of saying 'clean shreddies'), then clearly you have to change (and not just your pants). The first thing you could

---

[36] Provided that direction is the way to the toilet, you dirty bugger. You do realise, don't you, that skid marks become harder and harder to explain as you get older?

change – and even a cursory glance in the bowl will confirm this – is your diet. Next time you go out on the lash, you might consider ending your night with the more traditional hamburger or kebab, rather than scoffing the three battered sausages and a pickled onion you clearly swallowed whole after closing time last night . . .

𝍖 Historical Context

The Turtlehead is a classic reclusive rune – a vulnerable centre protected by a hardy shell, popping out only occasionally to see whether the world has got any better – and the classic recluse is Howard Hughes. Aviator, industrialist, filmmaker, philanthropist, former England football captain,[37] Poet Laureate[38] and engineer,[39] Howard Hughes is one of modern history's great enigmas.

Hughes's achievements in aviation engineering and the funding of medical research are well documented – so we'd prefer to talk about Jane Russell's tits. It seems that while filming *The Outlaw* in 1941, Hughes became obsessed with the appearance of Jane Russell's breasts. (And, having spent half an hour of our time and the best part of a box of Kleenex perusing Google Images, we can well understand why. Yowzer!). If we're reading our research material correctly (and we've got to admit that the pictures may well have distracted us from the words), Howard Hughes invented the world's first push-up bra. Now *that's* an invention.

Howard Hughes: we, the right-thinking men of the world, salute you!

---

[37] I think you'll find that's *Emlyn* Hughes. – Ed.
[38] And that's *Ted* Hughes. Bit more care in the research, do you think? – Ed.
[39] That's better. Thank you. – Ed.

Inverted

Ironically enough, for a rune that is so much about a tiny head poking out from a larger body, when you invert The Turtlehead you get a mushroom. But not just any mushroom: this one has an enormous head supported by the thinnest of stalks – a bit like Boris Johnson.[40] This is very different from The Turtlehead and it signifies a correspondingly different issue for you: if you eat too many mushrooms, your shit will turn black and smell so bad that you will fear you are shitting through the Devil's own arsehole. No word of a lie. We promise we're not just saying that because we hate vegetarians.

---

[40] Except . . . you know . . . smarter.

The Frenchman

Quick Reading

It may seem as if there's no problem that can't be dealt with or made light of with an ineffable Gallic shrug, although, of course, that doesn't solve everything. But don't despair. Sometimes it's just a case of '*merde* happens'.

Rites of Passage

Calm & Serene

Ah, the culture just drips off you, doesn't it, you suave bastard? Or is that sweat? Never mind; the point is that you have cultivated an air of sophistication and *élan* and everybody thinks you're the *chien's testicules*. *Très bon!*

Sound & Fury

Oh, cher! Wearing berets, eating garden pests and saying 'Va va voom' doesn't make you a sophisticate, no matter what the weekend supplements might say. It makes you a twat. Stop it at once.

What Did You Eat?

If you're taking this at all seriously, the answer is: loads of crap no right-thinking human being has any business having in his house, let alone putting in his mouth. Snails? Seriously? Frogs' legs? *Foie gras*? Tripe? Blue cheese? That's just got to be one of those jokes at our expense, hasn't it? Behind the kitchen door at any French restaurant is a gaggle of giggling Frenchmen, sniggering, '*Regardez le rosbif!* You can make zem eat anything just by saying it's a delicacy!'

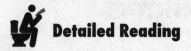 **Detailed Reading**

Zut, alors! There's a certainly an element of *je ne sais quoi* about you that fosters an easygoing *joie de vivre*. Problems are met with a shrug of the shoulders and a glass of red wine. No matter where you were born, at this point in time you have the heart and soul of The Frenchman. You poor bastard.

Of course, there are certainly advantages to your new Gallic insouciance. Even if your knowledge of French culture doesn't extend much beyond Kronenbourg 1664 and late-night 'art' films on Channel Five, your new interest in poetry, art, philosophy and losing wars will take you to places you didn't even know existed.

The downside is that you'll be quite incapable of making quick and rational decisions. Even the simplest choice will require hours of existential deliberation, the net result of which will ultimately lead you to conclude that life is a meaningless charade and that your time would best be spent drinking cognac and writing misogynistic poetry. But, when you get through the third pack of Gauloises, hopefully you'll snap out of it, jump in the shower and get back to normal. Either way, you might want to warn your friends that you'll be talking *merde* for a while.

What Action Can I Take?

Oh, *qui sons*? Who cares? It's all pointless, isn't it? Drink strong espresso, smoke like a dragon with a chest infection, read ridiculously long books about nothing at all – you're just going to die, anyway. You could try expressing your artistic side by curating an exhibition in your Loovre. Alternatively, since the French are known for their love of jazz, why not take the time to enjoy some top-notch scatting? Whatever you do, just do it quietly and leave us alone to contemplate the unbearable lightness of being . . .[41]

Historical Context

Internationally recognisable French icon? Wears ridiculous clothes? Capable of annoying the fuck out of people without even speaking? Why, it must be that poster boy for quintessentially Gallic *faux*-artistic irritating twats, Marcel Marceau.

But here we hit a problem. We were surprised to learn during our research that Marcel Marceau and his brother were actually war heroes. They joined the French Resistance in their late teens, rescued Jewish children from concentration camps and enlisted in Charles de Gaulle's Free French forces, where Marcel served as a liaison with Patton's American army, because of his excellent command of English.

We were further surprised to find ourselves both unable and unwilling to make fun of such heroism, so we must content ourselves with a simple observation: that 'walking against the wind' routine – what a load of *taureau merde*, eh?

---

[41] Yeah, of being a wanker.

Inverted

Appropriately enough, given the 'Historical Context' above, The Frenchman, when inverted, becomes The Thought Balloon (or *Ballon de pensée*). And a thought balloon, as everyone knows, signifies things that *aren't being said*. They could be things like 'Fucking hell! Look at the tits on that!' or 'Christ Almighty, did you cook this or shit it out after a long illness?' or even 'You know, it's funny: no matter how hard a poo might *feel* when it's splitting your sphincter on the way out, it's actually quite squishy if you bend it.'

The important thing is that you must never say them. Never.

The Hag

Quick Reading

An old woman is giving you the stink-eye. Beware her gaze and avoid her curse. And perhaps – and this is only a suggestion – try taking a dump in somebody else's front garden on the way home from the pub.

 Rites of Passage

Calm & Serene

The Hag is a symbol of feminine power and ancient magicks. You shouldn't be afraid of embracing your womanly side – after all, you sat down to produce *that*, didn't you?

Sound & Fury

Curses, black magic, warts – you know what this signifies, don't you? Yes, the mother-in-law is coming to visit. That's your cue to try grossing the old bat out with some spectacularly offensive turds.

What Did You Eat?

This is an interesting metaphysical conundrum, for it can be interpreted two ways: metaphorically and causally. Or, to be more in keeping with the essence of the book, how could the insipid mush an old hag stuffs in her gob possibly produce such a precise pattern of obviously rigid faeces?

Think about it. What does your average hag actually eat? If we view all that stuff about gingerbread houses and roast children as the nonsense it plainly is, we're left with one very simple answer, which is *I don't know but I bet it doesn't have much in the way of bones*. Of course, being the toothless

wonders of society, hags exist mainly on a diet of mushy peas and other people's sick.[42] But, in order to produce this particular rune, you'd need to swallow a whole frankfurter and the bottom half of an Action Man. So, what can it mean?

Sorry, but we can't tell you. Keeping secrets is a woman's prerogative.

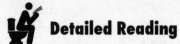 ## Detailed Reading

Traditionally, The Hag represents a witch or wise woman, but more modern interpretations can include any sort of healer, be it doctor, nurse, homeopath or masseuse. If you come into contact with any of these types, be sure to act pleasantly to them or suffer the potential ignominy of their evil eye. Or their evil fingers, as they wrench your testicles into positions no gonad was meant to occupy. Clearly, the appearance of this rune indicates that there are some seriously dark magicks working at the moment, and you should tread carefully.

But, even if you're having issues with a member of the distaff side, all is not lost. She may not *necessarily* be a force of supernatural evil. Even if she is, just as witches were often judged on the ducking stool, so too can this rune be evaluated by a simple rule: if The Hag sinks, then the woman in question is mortal and you're safe. If it floats, be prepared to deal with one seriously pissed-off witch.

---

[42] I can't wait to see the research documentation for *this* one. – Ed.

What Action Can I Take?

Unfortunately, the traditional methods of defeating a witch – e.g. pushing them into the oven or cutting their heads off with an axe – tend to be frowned upon by the more fussy of the modern judiciary, so that leaves us with a challenge. If, as per the 'Sound & Fury' section above, your problem really is with your mother-in-law, then we heartily endorse the method already set out: fill yourself with curry, kebabs and strong lager and produce as disgraceful array of rancid turds as you can without killing yourself in the process[43] and see if that scares the old bag off. For extra effectiveness, 'forget' to flush.

If the problem is with a woman of the non-familial variety, you can try to wait it out in the hope that she might get tired and go away, but they're stubborn beasts when they set their minds to it, so you may need a Plan B. To wit, you must pretend that:

- farts *aren't* funny;
- football *isn't* important;
- what she has to say *is* both relevant and worth listening to.

If nothing else, it ought to confuse the fuck out of her.

Historical Context

This was a difficult one, frankly. We had a very simple choice of two people who absolutely represent everything The Hag is and stands for. One of them is a politician of recent memory, very much alive and, therefore, capable of legal action against us; the other is a figure out of Slavic folklore. Being the cowardly, nervous pair we are, we chose the legendary Slavic witch, Baba Yaga.

---

[43] Or having your wife file for divorce on humanitarian grounds.

Baba Yaga, as we're sure everyone knows, first came to prominence as leader of the Conservative Party in 1975, after stabbing her mentor in the back, and rose to the post of prime minister four years later. Over the course of a decade and a half, she famously disenfranchised the poor, repressed the working classes, used the police force as her own private army, stole little children's milk and entered into a sordid affair with a senile old fuckwit from the New World, who thought he was a cowboy.

Oh, yeah. And she flew about the countryside in a giant mortar and lived in a house that moved about on chicken feet. True.

Inverted

Although it may look like a completely different rune and you might, therefore, expect a completely different reading, I'm afraid we're going to have to disappoint you. The Hag, when inverted, is very clearly a V-Neck Sweater or a Cardigan. And who, ladies and gentlemen of the jury, is by far the most likely person to give you a V-neck sweater or a cardigan and insist that you wear it? That's right: your gran, your mother-in-law, your senile auntie . . . in short, The Hag. The prosecution rests.

The Cat

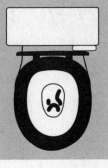

Quick Reading

Some things just can't be fixed. Bury your crap and walk away. If you've got time to preen in the process, more power to you!

 Rites of Passage

Calm & Serene

Oh, you are just *way* too cool. Moving gracefully, hunting perfectly, doing what you please when you please to almost universal acclaim. What a life!

Sound & Fury

What? No. Fuck off! *You* do it. I'm busy lying in the sun, licking my privates. What a life!

What Did You Eat?

If you're being true to The Cat, you've probably eaten a bewilderingly awful range of crap, while simultaneously turning your nose up at perfectly reasonable offerings. Just think about the stuff your average moggy eats – dead rats, pigeons' heads, frogs, snails, pieces of unidentified-but-revolting-smelling rodents – only to turn its back on £3-a-tin cat food. Picky little bastard.

The likelihood is that you've been stuffing your face full of fast-food burgers, fish and chips, kebabs filled with that rancid sausage-meat thing, pizzas, vindaloos and half-cooked pies, but, when your Significant Other offers you a home-cooked meal of pork chops and veggies, you sniff that it's 'not what I feel like' and start rifling through the takeaway menus.

The Cat

You know what? You don't *deserve* a home-cooked meal.
You deserve exactly what you've left in the bowl: a chunk
of unfeasibly shaped plop that looks like a cat taking a piss
against a wall.

 Detailed Reading

Felines are contradictory creatures and the one currently
lurking in your toilet bowl is no exception. While these runes
usually urge you to take responsibility for your actions, The
Cat says it's all right to sweep things under the carpet[44]
in order to move on, as long as you're sure that nobody
will ever find the mess you left behind. It's not that the
turd itself is so shameful: what really frightens you is the
embarrassment of its ever being found.

That's because, more than anything, cats value their
appearance. While this usually manifests itself as vanity,
there are other facets that you would do well to consider.
Think about the 'gifts' cats bring in for their owners. Dead
mice and the like may not be everyone's cup of tea, but to
the cat these are thoughtful and considerate gifts.

'What the fuck's *that* supposed to mean?' you may well ask.
Well, remember those presents you bought last year that
were received in what you thought was a less-than-effusive
manner? The power tools for the missus? The season ticket
for your seventy-year-old mum? The subscription to *Playboy*
for your gay mate at work?[45] You don't think any of these
could be construed as being just a *little* self-serving . . . ?

---

[44] Please tell us you realise this is a figure of speech. We really can't
overemphasise the gonad-endangering aspect of taking this at face value.

[45] And didn't it piss you off when he kept every issue? Turns out you *can*
actually read them for the articles.

With the wisdom of this rune freshly interpreted and bearing this in mind, it's probably best not to go gift shopping while The Cat has its claws in you. Play it safe and buy a book token, lest you have another mess that needs clearing up.

 ## What Action Can I Take?

Let's face it, 'action' and The Cat don't exactly go together, do they? If you've dropped this particular rune, your choices pretty much come down to a withering glance that combines arrogant scorn with a kind of accusative confession ('Yes, I did leave that shit in the bowl – and isn't it just like *you* to try to make something of it?'), and the tried and tested 'bury it and walk away' option.

Quite frankly, neither of those choices covers you in glory, so perhaps you should think twice about looking quite so fucking smug.

 ## Historical Context

There are many great cats through the ages, but rather than focus on Dick Whittington's cat, Puss in Boots or Cat Stevens, we've decided to go for the supreme ruler of them all – namely, the Egyptian cat goddess Bast. Worshipped in lower Egypt, Bast was goddess of the sun, of war and protector of the pharaoh and was worshipped by thousands of followers in a cult surrounding the ancient city of Bubastis.

Now *there's* a cat that has a right to feel superior!

Inverted

The inverted Cat is, somewhat appropriately, The Spanking. Take a look at your reeking rune. Tell me that's not a public schoolboy on his first year in senior school, bent over with his hands clasped together in supplication, screaming 'Thank you, sir, may I have another?' in a squeaky, prepubescent howl.[46] And who would be administering such a spanking? The only thing smugger than a cat – namely the head boy, a senior prefect who seems to enjoy punishing younger boys just a little too much . . .

[46] I don't know which one of you wrote this bit but, seriously, guys, you need some professional help. – Ed.

The Cow

Quick Reading

Moooooooo.

 Rites of Passage

Calm & Serene

You're totally at peace with the world – listening to the wind rustle through the trees while you enjoy the experience of simply *being*.

Sound & Fury

You are a brain-dead moron – listening to the crickets chirping in your head while you enjoy the experience of being simple.

What Did You Eat?

It's like this: cows eat grass; cows are ruminants (meaning they chew and digest their food many times – not that they regularly contemplate the great mysteries of existence). Cows are happy.[47] Proceeding from the deployment of this rune, it naturally follows that inner peace will come from eating like a cow. This doesn't mean throwing up back into your mouth – cows have four stomachs and are custom-designed for this – it just means take your time and enjoy your food, rather than just bolt down whatever ready meal had a reduced-price tag because it's perilously close to the best-before date.

---

[47] Well, they don't appear *unhappy*, do they? That's got to be a good start.

Detailed Reading

As well as producing prodigious pats, The Cow symbolises a certain . . . well . . . slowness to your actions at the moment. Don't be surprised if you find yourself staring into space for long periods at a time, vacantly chewing the cud or whatever passes for it. It's fine to take some time to clear your mind, but you may come to realise that someone is taking advantage of you while your brain is elsewhere. If you do find that someone is trying to milk you against your will, you may not be able to stop them – such is the compliant nature of The Cow.

Luckily, you're not alone. There's a whole herd of brainless bovines around you and, once you put the wind up them, you could find yourself at the head of a stampede. Just make sure you're not all running through the open gates to the abattoir.

What Action Can I Take?

That really depends on you. Some people like the herd instinct – it's safe, it means you're never alone and most of your decisions are made for you. If this sounds like you, then do nothing. It will keep you content and means there are more opportunities for the rest of us (you know, the ones who don't view their brains as optional extras).

If, on the other hand, you find yourself stampeding with the herd towards an unknown fate and want to slow down and smell the roses, then you need to do something, and do it now. You *could* exert your willpower and make a conscious effort to take control of your life – but we'd recommend sitting down to a nice meal of rump steak and French fries.

The Cow

Nothing says 'I'm finished with the old crowd' like eating their arse with chips.

🏛 Historical Context

Stomach full of grain? Paraded meekly to a certain end? Butchered in a horrific fashion? Sounds like Lindow Man, to us.

Discovered in a bog[48] in Cheshire, in 1984, Lindow Man is the most famous example of the 'bog body'. Found throughout the peat bogs of northern Europe, Great Britain and Ireland, these bodies are generally accepted to be the remains of human sacrifices to appease the gods, although there are a number of conflicting views currently gaining prominence. Definitely *not* among them is the assertion by local Manchester hard man Mad Kenny McGee, who claims to have battered Lindow Man to death for the heinous crime of 'spilling my pint'.

Inverted

The cow is a difficult rune to invert, as the three 'dots' representing teats are difficult to ascribe to any other naturally occurring phenomenon. While it's said that good things come in threes, it's difficult to find many trios that occur in nature. That leads us to the conclusion that what occurs in an inverted Cow rune is wholly unnatural and we are therefore forced to identify it as The Freak – signifying that whatever's happening at the moment runs contrary to the laws of nature.

---

[48] As in 'wetland', not khazi.

The Cow

Think carefully – do you have an extra nipple, nostril or nut? Was your mother's beard more lustrous than your father's? Have you ever felt inclined to hammer nails into your head or contort yourself into a large whisky bottle?[49] If the answer is 'yes' and you find yourself strangely out of place among normal folk, you might want to think about joining up when the circus is next in town.

Warning

One thing you should bear in mind when assessing this rune is that cows have been known to suffer epidemics of bovine spongiform encephalopathy – better known to the world as BSE or mad-cow disease. If you're concerned that you might have been exposed to this illness, you should immediately Moo! *Moooo*! Ha ha ha ha ha *ha ha*! I've got twelve heads on my foot and a bum full of soy milk! Ha ha ha ha ha ha *ha*! *Mooooooooooooooooooooo*!

---

[49] Other than in moments of extreme self-loathing and/or having just been dumped by a girlfriend?

The Rooster

Quick Reading

Why, that's quite a swagger you've got there, friend. Could it be you're trying a little too hard to convince us you're the pride of the hen house? Or is there a more ... medical reason for that ridiculous strut?

 ## Rites of Passage

Calm & Serene

Proud, virile, confident – The Rooster is a man among men. Or, if he's doing it right, a man among women.

Sound & Fury

Always crowing but doing precious little of what might actually be termed work, you talk the talk, sir, but you cannot walk the walk.[50]

What Did You Eat?

Obviously, a fair amount of poultry could have been consumed to make The Rooster, but there's also the possibility that you've been consuming products that might help increase your manliness. Powdered rhino horn with a Viagra chaser, perhaps?

---

[50] Presumably because this particular rune has left your bumhole in tatters and your trendy jeans are starting to chafe.

Detailed Reading

Well, well, well – who's that handsome devil strutting through life? Why, paint me pink and ride me to the Mardi Gras – it's you! Who would have thought that someone could have such manly confidence without any real basis for it? And therein lies the secret of The Rooster. You can strut around the place, chest out, bum out, groin a-wobbling, because the unnatural shape of your shit tells you that you, sir, are the cock of the walk.

And, as Top Man, this is a great time to start on new ventures, particularly ones with a high level of personal interaction. Such is your charm level at the moment that you'll be able to talk your way into (or out of) anything. The Rooster is a potent symbol in more ways than one, so don't be surprised if you catch the attention of potential partners. Success has its downsides, however. Remember that there's a fine line between confidence and arrogance. Everyone respects the spirit and self-assurance of a cock; but nobody likes a dick.

 What Action Can I Take?

Arsetrologically speaking, your best strategy to take advantage of The Rooster is to go at it like cock at a rival. You've got to have the balls to make hard decisions and the spunk to stick to them. Don't let yourself get shafted – if you allow a challenger to grab you by the short-and-curlies, you could find yourself spent before the climax. The competition is sure to be stiff but, touch wood, you can keep the vigour injected by The Rooster coming for long enough to see the job through to the finish.

⚏ Historical Context

Hmm . . . full of self-importance, lord of all he surveys, name unfortunately similar to a set of reproductive organs. Sounds a lot like King Cnut, to us. This famous Danish king – also known as 'Canute' to those cowardly historians who want to reduce the chance of a catastrophic typo appearing in their work – ruled over large swathes of Denmark, England and Scandinavia, early in the eleventh century.

Canute's many political and military successes made him one of the great figures of medieval European history. But, despite his manifold and legitimate claims to fame, this historical Rooster figure is best known for the overweening pride that compelled him to stand on the beach and command the tide not to come in. The tide, of course, refused, and ran up the beach, wetting his feet and the bottom of his robe. He is reputed to have reacted by throwing all his toys out of the pram, including his crown, which he never wore again. What a cnut!

The Rooster

Inverted

When inverted, The Rooster forms a shape that will perhaps be more familiar to our British readers than those in other, less civilised parts of the world[51] – namely, The Bowler in the classic follow-through pose. This occurs immediately after the ball has been released but before the bowler is able to regain equilibrium, come to a halt and – if he's Australian – raise impertinent questions regarding the batsman's parentage, sexuality and ability to wield a cricket bat. Hmm, not all that different from The Rooster, after all. Still a bit of a cock.

---

[51] We're looking at you, America. You can't carry on playing sports that no one else takes an interest in and then calling yourself 'world champions'. You have to give sport to the world, as we did. And then let everyone else get better at it and thrash you every chance they get. As we did.

The Anchor

Quick Reading

Drop some ballast to prevent being flushed away by the current. Oh, wait, you already did that. Listen, this 'anchor'... it's not still ... *connected* ... is it?

 Rites of Passage

Calm & Serene

Nothing but blue skies here. You are one of the lucky few who know where their calm harbour is, and, consequently, your life is secure, stable and balanced. You smug prick.

Sound & Fury

Oh, dear! It's quite likely you wake up every morning feeling like a shipwreck: one mast still standing, all hands on deck and seamen running everywhere.

What Did You Eat?

Unless you want to die of scurvy, some limes should be top of your list. It's a little-known fact that the strange configuration of The Anchor owes much of its formation to the complete excretion of all vitamin C from the digestive system. Those two straight plops represent the last vestiges of your body's vitamin C and the bendy one represents what happens to your bones when you get scurvy.[52]

---

[52] Or, if you want to be slave to the tyranny of facts, it's what happens to your bones when you contract rickets, which is caused by a deficiency of vitamin D, not C. But why let medical science get in the way of a tenuous spiritual metaphor?

In keeping with advice elsewhere in this section, we would counsel you not to eat anything that can be joined together to form any sort of chain in your stomach. No spaghetti, linguini, fettuccine or other ropelike foods.

Detailed Reading

Mighty waters are raging around you, but don't worry because The Anchor will provide you with some much needed stability. Even though the seas are choppy, rest assured that you won't be dragged away with the tide. All you have to do is hold on. Once the storm has passed, it'll be plain sailing. For the moment, though, you'd best wait for the all-clear.

But beware! There's an old nautical saying: an anchor is only as strong as the chain that holds it, and a chain is only as strong as its weakest link. So, while you may be relying on friends and family to hold you together during this difficult time, you have to ask yourself whether they're really the people you can rely on.

Everybody's got a mate who's a little bit . . . out there. You know the one we're talking about. The one who's prone to taking his trousers off in the middle of the pub. The one who's most likely to say, 'Fuck it, let's *snort* the vodka and see what that's like.' The one who laminates copies of *TV Quick* and doesn't like to talk about it. Is this the person you want to rely on to keep you safe? Is this your anchor? Or just a wanker?

🧻 What Action Can I Take?

Before we can answer that question, there's a couple of physiological matters that we need to clear up. So, besides sentiment, is there anything . . . you know . . . *organic* that's tying you to this particular rune? If there is some kind of scatological umbilical cord joining your shite to your small intestine, then whatever you do, *don't flush*. Unseemly as it might, er, seem, we think your only option is to 'weigh anchor' (so to speak) and head down to the A&E[53] department for some competent medical help. Otherwise you'll be dragged down the S-bend and through the sewage system, as a sidekick to your own shit.

🏛 Historical Context

Because he's safely almost three hundred years dead and, therefore, can't (a) sue us or (b) jam a cutlass up our backsides, we have no hesitation in declaring the quintessential historical avatar of The Anchor to be none other than Edward Teach, better known to the world as Blackbeard.

Scourge of the Caribbean Sea during the early eighteenth century, Blackbeard is regarded as the archetypal image of the seafaring pirate. Loaded down with cutlasses and with his bandolier stuffed full of pistols, Blackbeard was a source of terror for honest sailors. Legend has it that he had cannon fuses and lit matches braided into his beard before battle, to intimidate his enemies further. It's also said that the idea of pirates burying treasure has its origins with Blackbeard, who used to go ashore in a small boat, with a chest full of

---

[53] Arse traumas & Exit wounds.

treasure and a single sailor to help bury it – although he would inevitably return alone. Huh. Now *there's* a shit job . . .

Inverted

In keeping with the historical precedent above, inverting The Anchor gives you the tree – the item most often used as a marker for buried treasure. That's not to say that *every* tree has a chest of dubloons buried at the foot, but who's to say for sure? Head to the local arboretum (or, more likely, your local garden centre or public park) with a spade and a bag marked swag and it could all be yours! Yo-ho-ho and a bottle of rum.

The Snail

Quick Reading

You're carrying a heavy load and leaving a smear behind you – but you'll get there in the end. Of course, you could always take something to speed up the action. Maybe some salts . . . Er, hang on!

Rites of Passage

Calm & Serene

You enjoy the nomadic lifestyle, and who could blame you? Always seeing new sights, never tied down for too long – and if one of us had left something like *that* in the bowl, we'd want to leave the scene of the crime pretty sharpish, too.

Sound & Fury

It's such a burden carrying your world around on your back the way you do. Hey, maybe it was all that extra weight that made you squirt out the weird Mr Whippy of a turd.

What Did You Eat?

This classic juxtaposition of straight shit and curly crap (which is, by a startling coincidence, the name of a very successful 1970s comedy duo, who specialised in scatological humour[54]), means that your diet is pretty balanced – as far as what *comes out* is concerned, anyway. Christ knows what's *gone in*. If you're leaving a shitty snail trail everywhere, you've got some nutritional issues to deal with that we're not really qualified to advise you on. The main point to remember here is that some foods are

---

[54] No, it isn't. Stop fucking about, you two. – Ed.

supposed to be crunchy on the outside and soft on the inside – pies, for instance – and others . . . Well, it's as clear a 'past its used-by date' message as Mother Nature is able to provide. And the fact that this also perfectly describes the physical condition of a two-week-old dog turd should be taken as a warning – not an amusing coincidence.

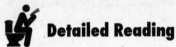 ## Detailed Reading

There's a general sense of torpor enveloping you at the moment, but appearances can be deceptive. While it's certainly true that you're not going to be winning the sprint, there's steady progress being made. Down the inside of your trouser legs, for instance.

One of the main things that is slowing you down is the amount of baggage you're carrying around. No one could blame you for wanting to cast off this burden and making a dash for it, but to do so would be a huge mistake. Your possessions provide security and reassurance and to throw them away needlessly would lead to disaster. There's no guarantee you'd move faster, anyway – and, frankly, we wouldn't be in a screaming hurry to put any undue pressure on a backside that's just shat *that* out.

What Action Can I Take?

Well, the first thing you can do is avoid salty foods. The Snail is one of the more literal of the Arsetrological runes, and, while exposure to salt won't prove as harmful to you as it would to a snail or slug, it won't half make your shit fizz. You've had a big night out and woken up the next morning feeling like death warmed up, right? Downstairs for a pint of water with a soluble aspirin? Feels all fizzy and funny going down, doesn't it? Ever wonder what it would feel like at the other end of the equation?

Historical Context

While The Snail is notable for its slow movements, the greater historical context can be attained by looking at the nomadic principle of carrying your possessions around with you. The best known of the nomadic peoples are the Gypsies, so that's where we've chosen to focus our attention. And it may well surprise you to learn that the most famous of all the Gypsies was one Sir Charles Spencer Chaplin, better known to the world as Charlie. Well, all right, one of his grandmothers was half-Romany so, technically, Chaplin was only one-eighth Gypsy, but that's good enough for us.

Moving around continually as a child, Chaplin lived in a variety of homes and was, in fact, extremely proud of his Romany heritage. Remember the Little Tramp's funny waddling walk that charmed the world? You can't tell us that's not the stride of a man who's just launched a little something into his trousers.

The Snail

Inverted

Ha! This is an easy one. The Snail, when inverted, becomes The Whistle. The interpretation is quite straightforward: either something's making you jump, or you're waiting for a signal to let you know you can get moving. Whichever way you choose to look at it, your response should be the same: take control of your life. You don't need to be startled by anything, nor do you need anyone's permission. Just do it.

Oh, and, if your arse does actually make a whistling sound when you shit, see a doctor. You've punctured your small intestine.

The Crocodile

Quick Reading

Beware of innocent-looking logs – they may turn around to bite you.

 ## Rites of Passage

Calm & Serene

Death floats at the surface of the pool, waiting to take the unwary to a watery grave. Can you *really* tell the difference between your unfeasibly symmetrical plop and nature's perfect killing machine?[55]

Sound & Fury

They never blink, you know. So silent, so shiny, so . . . brown. Unchanged through millions of years of evolution, the comically shaped turd is as funny now as it must have been to our Neanderthal ancestors.[56]

What Did You Eat?

Crocodiles have particularly unsavoury eating habits – they take their prey under the water, savage the victim until they die and then store them in a 'meat locker' until they go slightly rotten, at which point it's clearly dinner time. Far be it from us to suggest that your botty products are in a similar state of evil decay, but you don't honestly think this rune is the product of a healthy diet and clean living, do you?

---

[55] Probably. Australian news reports rarely speak of the tragedy of the young tourist who went swimming and was eaten by a four-metre length of shite.
[56] Or 'Millwall supporters' as they're sometimes known.

 **Detailed Reading**

The Crocodile is all about deception, so be wary of everything you see around you. Just as the floating log might turn out to be a murderous reptile, so too might that friendly stranger turn out to be your new worst enemy. Or that Lion Bar floating in the swimming pool may turn out to be . . . you know . . . *not* a Lion Bar.

We all know the saying about crocodile tears, so don't be fooled by a dramatic performance. Good actors know how to manipulate their audience, so maintain a healthy air of cynicism to any histrionics that are sent in your direction. If you've learned just one thing from reading this book, you should have learned how to recognise shit when you see it. That said, be careful about expressing your disbelief. Even if there are creatures moving against you, it might not be a wise idea to let them know that you're on to them. Sometimes the best way to survive is to stay still and let the predator pass by in search of other prey.[57]

 What Action Can I Take?

Would it be cowardly or glib to suggest running like fuck?

Actually, there is a very effective strategy for dealing with The Crocodile, and all it really requires from you is the wit to see your situation for what it is, early enough. You see, although a crocodile can bite *down* with an incredible pressure approaching 5,000 pounds per square inch, the muscles that *open* the jaw are actually relatively weak. Just as an adult male could probably hold a crocodile's jaw shut (a useful technique if only he could also deal with

---

[57] However, we feel we should point out that this is also an excellent way to be eaten without even putting up a fight. Mother Nature's a bitch like that.

the razor-sharp claws and the almost 3,000 pounds of angry reptile), an astute Arsetrology buff can deal with the repercussions of The Crocodile with a minimum of effort, can he but see the problem coming early enough.

Historical Context

It goes without saying that, when we're talking about crocodiles, our most famous historical figure is Mick 'Crocodile' Dundee from the eighties masterpiece of the same name. While it's tempting to put yourself in his snakeskin boots and think that you're master of the outback, the truth is that cocking your head and going *mrrrrrwwwwng*, isn't going to do you much good. Nor will shagging Linda Kozlowski. (Mick's real-life counterpart, 'Crocodile Hunter' Steve Irwin, is deceased and we felt it would be in poor taste to mention him. Believe it or not, there are some depths that even *we* won't stoop to.)

Inverted

It should be plain to seasoned Arsetrologers and novices alike that what you get when you invert The Crocodile is . . . The Alligator. 'Wait a minute!' we hear you cry. 'That's just another word for a crocodile!'. Well, our ignorant friend, we beg to differ. The differences are numerous!

The alligator has a broad, shovel-like snout, whereas the crocodile's snout is a much sharper V shape. What's more, the crocodile's jaws are roughly the same size, so that, if you're stupid enough to get that close to them, you can see both their top and bottom teeth emerging from the jaw. The alligator, in contrast, has an upper jaw much wider than its lower jaw, resulting in an 'overbite' – just like that kid at high school with the Coke-bottle glasses that you and your friends used to tease for being a retard.

Look, the upshot of this impromptu lesson in crocodilian biology is that— All right. You win. They're the same, OK? And so are the poos. If you invert The Crocodile, you get The Alligator and it means exactly the same thing. You happy? Now leave us alone.

The Cradle

Quick Reading

With a bit of pushing and straining, you can produce something beautiful.

 Rites of Passage

Calm & Serene

Aw! Isn't that cute? He's got your eyes. No . . . wait . . . those are bits of sweetcorn.

Sound & Fury

You know how much pain, frustration and swearing results from trying to assemble flat-packed furniture? Now imagine holding the Allen key with your arse.

🍔 What Did You Eat?

Did you know that some cultures eat the afterbirth? Well, they do – but that's not really advisable here.

On a marginally more tasteful note, it should be recognised that The Cradle is a rune chock-full of contradictions.[58] The nature of a cradle is that it is a solid, rigid structure – designed as it is for keeping a baby cosy and safe. But the nature of a baby is that it can eat only soft, mushy food. Can this be so? Can a sloppy, mushy meal produce turds of such a firm nature? Not if our experiences with chicken vindaloo are anything to go by, so clearly we need to seek another answer.

---

[58] And corn. Did we mention the corn?

It is here that the awesome power of Arsetrology comes into its own, for surely the passing of a plop like this can only be due to arcane forces. Or swallowing a Meccano set.

 ## Detailed Reading

Perhaps the only thing people get more squeamish about than going to the toilet is the process of childbirth. You don't have the luxury of averting your eyes or fainting, however, as the appearance of The Cradle indicates that you are (at least metaphorically) delivering something new into the world.

This isn't necessarily an actual baby but it *is* something wonderful and extraordinary. Of course, you need to be aware that, no matter how beautiful this 'thing' may be, the delivery process will not be an easy affair. You'll have to be patient during the gestation period and then summon all your mental and physical strength to push it out. But, once it arrives, everything will be different. For all the challenges that have been and for all those that lie ahead, take some time to acknowledge the beauty of the new creation you hold in your hands.[59]

---

[59] And, just in case you didn't read the introduction, we're going to reiterate that you shouldn't be handling anything from the toilet bowl. It's a metaphor. Met-a-phor.

What Action Can I Take?

The traditional response to The Cradle is to call for hot water and clean towels – presumably because there are some things even double-quilted toilet paper can't deal with. The real key to deciding what to do in response to The Cradle is to answer this question honestly: am I trying to do something new? If the answer is yes, congratulations! For The Cradle says your venture is almost certain to be successful. Who says you can't polish a turd?

If the answer to the question is no, however, you're in for a rather unpleasant surprise. Because *something's* emerging from the bum lips of life and it's got its beady eye on *you*.

 Historical Context

The selection of a historical figure to represent The Cradle is a difficult one – there are surprisingly few famous babies. However, once the criteria are broadened to include birth and motherhood, the problem resolves itself quite neatly: Sigmund Freud. At first glance, the father of modern psychology might seem an odd choice. However, the rumpled, ~~penis~~ cigar-smoking Austrian *did* give birth to a new branch of medicine, making him both appropriate and too clever by half. And he also tended to trace all of your problems back to sex or your mother – preferably both – thereby making him exactly the sort of fucked-up individual who would likely be proud to be associated with a book about shit.

Inverted

What happens when you invert The Cradle? Well, the child is trapped – made prisoner by the bars that were supposed to keep it safe. Needless to say, this is probably going to have the child welfare officer knocking on your door, ready to haul you into court. As if that weren't bad enough, the tabloids will probably name you 'THE DEVIL DADDY' and, when you're sent down for child cruelty, you'll probably get shivved with a sharpened toothbrush. So, if you get an inverted Cradle, it's best to maximise your caring side, or reap the whirlwind.

The Temple

Quick Reading

It's time to find your spiritual centre. Best lock the door and concentrate.

 Rites of Passage

Calm & Serene

In the hustle and bustle of modern life, it's important to take some time to contemplate higher things. And get some quality magazine reading in.

Sound & Fury

Of course, it's difficult to meditate when there's someone banging on the door, asking how long you're going to be.

What Did You Eat?

Given The Temple's shape and uncanny resemblance to Stonehenge, we'll forgo the obvious explanation (three chipolatas) and go for a nice metaphor, namely a human sacrifice. Of course, we don't *literally* mean a human being ritually murdered to ensure the harvest is plentiful. No, no – any old dead body will do. You could frequent road accidents, get a job at the local morgue or even take up grave robbing. It doesn't matter how you appease The Temple – the important thing is to find a dead body and tuck in![60]

---

[60] I'm not even *trying* to keep you out of trouble any more. You're on your own. – Ed.

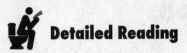

Detailed Reading

It's time to shut yourself away from the world and take some time to regain your inner balance. In today's society it's all too easy to get lost in the commotion of modern society. The appearance of The Temple indicates that you need to find a tranquil place in which to restore your equilibrium. And, if there happens to be a well-thumbed copy of *Razzle* nearby to help you, um, meditate, then who are we to cast aspersions?

Let's not confine ourselves to the smallest room in the house, though – this idea of sanctuary can mean taking a trip away by yourself, finding the time to meditate or even something as simple as locking the bathroom door, pouring yourself a scented bath and lighting a couple of candles (if you're into that sort of thing, you big fairy). But, no matter where you seek your Temple, what's important is that you take some time for yourself.

With this accomplished, you'll be amazed at how much more relaxed you feel. By taking the time to remain still and calm, you'll be more able to cope with the stresses of modern life, and more attuned to the spiritual centre that is all too easy to neglect.

What Action Can I Take?

The Temple is indeed the yin and yang of poo runes. Your possible courses of action are very much defined by the 'Rites of Passage', above. If this one dropped out calm and serene, then you may want to consider taking a serious look at your spiritual priorities. Maybe Sunday mornings – currently a foul-smelling miasma of AGBs,[61] splitting headaches and hangover wanks – could be better spent contemplating the Lord. In this case, The Temple is a sign that your life is out of balance and you need to attend to the sacred as well as the sordid.

If, however, you birthed this particular turd through a crimson mist of sound and fury, it's likely a sign that religion has largely failed you and you should pursue a more pragmatic life strategy. A rune like The Temple *looks* as if it would hurt to produce and, unsurprisingly, it *did* hurt – *ergo*, we live in a rational world and must accept the consequences of our actions, rather than bleat for intercession by a supreme being. It's time to start taking responsibility for your own life and say goodbye to a life of church services. The altar wine was shit, anyway.

---

[61] AGB: After-Grog Bog. Don't pretend you don't know what we're talking about.

🏛 Historical Context

The biblical figure of Samson is for ever linked to this rune, having given his life to bring down the temple of the Philistines. What is less well known is the fact that he was – as well as a figure of Herculean strength and long, flowing locks – a serial killer of epic proportions.

To follow Samson's exploits in the Bible is to experience a litany of horrific murders, as Philistines are smashed, bashed, throttled and torn apart by this psychotic madman. Our (admittedly minimal) research indicates that Samson was personally responsible for the deaths of more than two thousand Philistines. He even killed a thousand in a single battle, using nothing but his jaw and his arse[62] – which is exactly the sort of behaviour you'd expect from someone whose bumhole had been torn apart in the passing of The Temple . . .

Inverted

What's the opposite of The Temple? The best our prurient minds could come up with was The Brothel, but, since this section is about the *shape* of the rune rather than the theme, it's with real regret that we state that this isn't a licence to visit the massage parlour and ask for a Bangkok sandwich with extra oil. If you invert The Temple you can plainly see that the result is The Container, the interpretation of which is quite straightforward: get your shit together.

---

[62] The *jawbone* of an *ass*. Come on, guys, we've talked about this – sort it out, will you? – Ed.

The Conundrum

Quick Reading

The Conundrum is where Zen philosophy and Arsetrology meet. What is the sound of one hand clapping? Who will guard the guardians? And, more to the point, what's brown and sticky?[63]

 ## Rites of Passage

Calm & Serene

There is a puzzle in your life, but rather than being a source of irritation, it's actually quite energising. Imagine the sense of achievement you'll feel when you solve it.

Sound & Fury

Yes, there's a puzzle in your life, all right, but the joke's on you. If someone's dropping a (hopefully) fake doggy doo in your desk drawer, don't get drawn into a prank war – the curly-shaped plop in your bowl is a sure sign that you're doomed to lose.

What Did You Eat?

The ineffable question to be asked after you've shat a question mark is: what *did* I eat? It's a riddle wrapped in a mystery inside an enigma and, rather than try to untangle it, The Conundrum is asking you to consider the other essential enigmas of our time, such as: if a bird in the hand is worth two in the bush, why do so many men crave threesomes? *Can* you polish a turd? And, if a bus travelling from London to Manchester moves at an average speed of sixty miles an

---

[63] A stick. Ha! It's not *all* about poo, you know.

hour, and a train travelling from Edinburgh to Manchester moves at an average speed of ninety miles an hour, does anybody really give a toss?

 ## Detailed Reading

It's very easy to take the view that these sorts of puzzles are simply meant to distract and confuse you. To this accusation, we respond 'Hmm? Oh, I'm sorry, I was miles away. What were you saying?'

A glib response, perhaps, but the fact of the matter is that, if you really want to understand The Conundrum, you're going to have to engage in some lateral thinking.

The manifestation of this rune indicates that there is a person, place or thing that you just can't get your head around. No matter how you look at it, this mystery defies categorisation and you could easily find yourself becoming obsessed with the problem rather than the solution. And the truth is that there are no problems, only opportunities.

But the further you get into it, the less likely you are to come up with a solution. Instead, take a step back. Only by looking at the whole picture will you be able to understand its meaning. Also: doesn't it smell a lot better from back here?

What Action Can I Take?

Are you a crossword king? A sudoku sorcerer? A tic-tac-toe . . . tosser? Then you're a lucky man, indeed. Not that those skills will help you solve The Conundrum, but at least you'll have something to keep you busy while the world unravels around you. Sadly, navigating the choppy waters of The Conundrum requires more than an affinity for word games or mathematical puzzles. You need to be able to see beneath this illusion we call life and understand the intrinsic structure of your dilemma. Put aside your prejudices and long-held opinions, and approach the problem from the other side. You can solve your dilemma only by applying common sense and logic rather than emotional reactions. Do that and it's a piece of cake. Oh, and flush that shit down the toilet, will you? It's scaring the children.

Historical Context

Who better to represent the impenetrable mystery of The Conundrum than the man who has been described variously as an adventurer, an alchemist, a courtier, an inventor, a musician and a composer? Ladies and gentlemen of the lavvy, I give you the Count of St Germain.

This mysterious eighteenth-century gentleman is a recurring figure in legend and literature, appearing in work by Alexander Dumas and Umberto Eco, among others. Although historical records seem to indicate that he enjoyed little more than his allotted three score years and ten, rumours persist that he is immortal. These stories have him doomed to walk the earth for ever, much like Michael Palin or the Wandering Jew.[64] Others maintain that he is a semi-mystical

---

[64] As in either/or, not a.k.a.

figure, having been frequently reincarnated, rather than ascribing his myth to immortality. These wackos believers claim that the Count of St Germain lived as Plato, Merlin, a high priest of Atlantis, Christopher Columbus and Saint Joseph (you know: Jesus's stepdad).

Need more convincing that this is a classic Arsetrological archetype? Look at it this way: have you ever heard a bigger pile of shit in your life?

Inverted

Invert The Conundrum and you get The Fat Bloke. No mysteries here. Stop eating so much and get some exercise, you gluttonous bastard.

The Pyramid

Quick Reading

You are capable of great works, but they require strenuous effort and monumental labour to produce.

 ## Rites of Passage

Calm & Serene

If you really believe in what you're doing, the result will be worth all of your efforts. Possibly.

Sound & Fury

You're far too impatient to finish your great work. If you don't put some protective procedures in place, many will die – and Health and Safety will shut down your arse.

What Did You Eat?

A pyramid is nothing without its riches – so eat well and eat hearty! If you make sure to cover all four major food groups,[65] you should be able to lay some sound foundations for your monument. If possible, you should try to match your eating to the structure of The Pyramid, so start with a large, flat base (a loaf of bread, say) and then work your way through smaller courses (leg of lamb, quarter-pounder, fish finger, mint) until you get all the way to The Pyramid's tip. At this point, you'll probably want to wrap yourself in bandages, lie down in a cool, dark place and not be disturbed for a few thousand years . . .

---

[65] Beer, pizza, crisps and curry.

 **Detailed Reading**

You're capable of constructing some mighty structures at the moment, and your vision is such that there is no limit to your ambition. But, while you may have the eyes of a pharaoh, you don't have the resources of one. Pyramids were constructed by armies of slaves, whereas your monument will be built of your own blood, sweat and tears. And shite.

This edifice upon which you lavish your efforts will require more personal sacrifice than Tutankhamun could ever dream of,[66] but, truly, you can't make an omelette without breaking a few eggs. Always remember, too, that you will have your knockers (chiefly on the door to the loo, asking when you're going to be finished and reminding you to use the air freshener this time), but your work is worth the effort. What you accomplish in this endeavour will be matched only by what you learn along the way. People may say that you're crazy to undertake such an ambitious project, but the vision in your head is complete. By all means listen to their advice, but don't let the naysayers distract you from the bigger picture.

And let no man mock your secret passage.

---

[66] As opposed to *personnel* sacrifice, with which he seemed quite familiar.

🧻 What Action Can I Take?

Just like the pharaohs, you should allow no one to stand in the way of your great project (not that anyone would be tempted – let's face it). 'Push, push, push' should be your mantra – although it may seem, to those listening in horror at the door, to sound more like 'Nnngh! Nnngh! Nnngh!'

Putting puerile *double entendres* aside,[67] The Pyramid is a clear sign that a mighty project is looming in your life – one that will command all of your energies and use up most of your resources. In order to ensure that this great work proceeds according to plan, feel free to behave like a complete and utter bastard.

Seriously, what's everyone else doing with their life? Trying to raise a family? Make the world a better place? Losers! They matter not. None of them has the courage you do: the courage to build a mighty monument to selfishness and ego – and, what's more, to build it out of shit.

Do as you please and let the ants scurry from your path, for *you* are Ozymandias, king of kings. Let a curse be laid on any who dare disturb the sanctity of your chamber.

🏛 Historical Context

This should come as no mystery. We weren't pissing about when we mentioned Ozymandias – the classic historical personage for The Pyramid is, of course, Ramses II. Regarded as the greatest of all the pharaohs, Ramses II ascended to the throne in his early twenties and ruled Egypt for more than sixty years – and bear in mind this was over three thousand years ago, when the average life span was about

---

[67] . . . would make this book twelve pages long. – Ed.

half an hour if you didn't annoy anyone bigger than you and fifteen minutes if you did. Truly, a remarkable achievement; one can only assume that his bowel movements were both regular and powerful.

Ramses II built extensively throughout Egypt, constructing such marvels of the ancient world as the temple at Abu Simbel, the monument known as the Ramesseum and the legendary city of Pi-Ramesses. Rumours that he also constructed a 500-foot-tall pyramid made only from the baked faeces of his wives and children – a structure that reeked so badly in the hot Egyptian summer that it was known throughout the land as 'The Stinx' – remain, alas, only rumours.

Inverted

It's a fascinating symmetry that the inverted Pyramid gives rise to The Beehive – we're sure the significance won't be lost on you. Just as scarabs were the sacred beetles[68] of the Egyptians, so are bees the . . . um— Oh my God! *Look!* A mummy! *Ruuuuuunnn!!!!!*

---

[68] This is actually true – and, what's more, it's all because of shit! The scarabs used to roll up balls of crap to lay their eggs in. Then, when new baby scarabs ate their way out, the ancient Egyptians thought it was the same scarab coming back to life, so they worshipped them. (You know, this is so close to the truth, I really can't be bothered taking issue. Well done, boys. You really know your shit. – Ed.)

The Nimbus

Quick Reading

Ever wonder exactly what a shit storm looks like?
Then just take a peek in the bowl ...

 Rites of Passage

Calm & Serene

Don't panic. Even the fiercest storms pass eventually. Take
adequate precautions, let the tempest pass over you, and get
on with your life.

Sound & Fury

'Even the fiercest storms pass eventually.' This is true – but
not much comfort if they take your roof with them. This is
going to be bad, so get your waterproofs out.

What Did You Eat?

This is a vital question where The Nimbus is concerned, and
the reasoning is refreshingly free of mysticism or metaphor.
If your diet conforms to what we broadly refer to as being
'balanced' – five-a-day fruit and veg, a nice mix of protein,
roughage and carbohydrates – and you take regular exercise,
then we're afraid this rune represents a serious omen (the
nature of which will be explained below).

If, on the other hand, your usual dining habits tend to take
in Mexican hot pizzas and beef vindaloo, washed down with
a generous amount of Château de Carlsberg, then we can
probably explain this particular poo without resorting to
supernatural causes, and the only advice we have to offer is
that you should be ashamed of yourself.

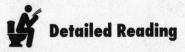

Detailed Reading

Notwithstanding the caveat above, we can safely say that the appearance of The Nimbus in your crapper means just one thing: there's a storm coming. And it looks like being a stinker.

Time to batten down the hatches and get the pets inside, because there's foul weather heading in your direction. You've felt the pressure building for some time – the atmosphere has been crackling with potential energy and now the storm is upon you. Mental, physical and spiritual bombardment combine to produce a flurry of negative energy.

But don't despair. It's important to realise that there is help available during this crisis – whether it's a friend, partner or your local clergyman, the important thing is to tell someone what's going on.[69]

Of course, if you answered 'beer and curry' to the diet question above, it's likely that all of this turmoil can be explained by the fact that you're hung over like a bastard. Either way, a bit of time spent indoors won't do you any harm.

What Action Can I Take?

What action can *anyone* take against the fury of the storm? Try to keep sheltered and dry. Ensure that you've made your goods and chattels secure. Recognise these forces that are aligned against you, respect their power, but do not be afraid to stand against them. And remember: it is better to bend with the wind and spring back than to break. And that would be profound guidance even if we *hadn't* got it out of a fortune cookie at the local Chinese last night.

---

[69] Although, to be honest, your local clergyman is unlikely to have much sympathy with your turning your back on the Lord and placing your faith in a cheap paperback about the predictive power of poo.

If you're in the hung-over category from the section above, the advice is pretty much the same, but with one small addition — eat some vegetables, for fuck's sake! You spray that turd tornado into the bowl, sit there gasping in the aftermath with your sphincter muscles flapping like shutters in a storm and you seriously want to tell us there's nothing amiss with your diet? What's *wrong* with you?

Historical Context

Who else could best embody The Nimbus but Thor, the Norse god of thunder?

Thor was, of course, the son of Odin, Lord of Asgard, and half-brother to Loki, the Norse god of mischief. A powerful warrior and an equally mighty carouser, Thor was a favourite deity of the Vikings. He was frequently called on to inspire victory in battle and was said to command the very storms themselves. According to legend, he fought and slew many giants, but was himself slain killing the world serpent Jormundgand, at Ragnarok, the fabled Twilight of the Gods.

Thor is perhaps best known for wielding the fabled hammer, Mjölnir, and it is this that makes him most appropriate for this rune. Because, if any turd in this book looks as if it's been smashed into a fine mist by a fucking great hammer, it's The Nimbus.

The Nimbus

Inverted

To be perfectly frank, inverting The Nimbus is a little like fucking a jellyfish – it's extremely difficult, leaves a God-awful mess and any satisfaction you might feel, should you somehow manage to succeed, is almost immediately replaced by an all-encompassing sense of shame. Or so we're told.

It's a little easier in Arsetrological terms, though (and a damn site less messy), where the opposite of a storm is a flood. So, when you invert The Nimbus you get The Deluge. The effects are pretty much the same as those described above, but the shit rises up through the floorboards, rather than leaking in through the ceiling.

The Moon

Quick Reading

You're in a crazy sort of mood at the moment.
Be careful what – and whom – you expose
yourself to.

 Rites of Passage

Calm & Serene

Don't be afraid to make use of a sudden rush of ideas. After
all, one man's madness is another man's genius.

Sound & Fury

You may think it's fun to flash the occasional moon, but,
when the police officer you've just honoured with your
cheeky salute reaches for the latex glove, 'It seemed like a
good idea at the time' is pretty cold comfort.

What Did You Eat?

The Moon, as everyone knows, is made of green cheese.
And any cheese that has turned green shouldn't be eaten,
should it? It's time to start checking the 'best before' dates
and clear out the fridge before a case of gastroenteritis
strikes. Some flannel-wearing macrobiotic killjoys will tell
you that the mouth is the dirtiest orifice on the body, but try
convincing them that sticking a spoon up your arse is just as
clean as putting a fork in your mouth and they can't quite
see the point. Either way, it's time to stop eating cheese
before bedtime.

 **Detailed Reading**

The word 'lunatic' derives from the Latin '*luna*' (meaning moon – duh!) and anecdotal evidence tells us the crime rate rises whenever the moon is in full ascension.[70] The appearance of The Moon in your toilet bowl, however, doesn't mean that you're going to turn into an insane axe murderer. (Although, it doesn't rule it out.)

Don't be surprised, however, if you find yourself having thoughts that are a little more colourful than usual. And by 'colourful' we mean 'batshit crazy'. The Moon is a symbol of unfettered creativity and it's possible to become quite giddy at the new ideas that hit you in the dead of night.

Wouldn't it be great to invent a coffee machine that starts brewing as soon as it detects your first fart of the morning? Why aren't newspapers printed on bread, so you can eat the headlines on the way to work? Why hasn't anyone made a conservatory out of cheese, so you can curl up on a sofa made of biscuits and cover yourself in port? You see? Crazy talk. You'd never eat a whole loaf of bread for breakfast.

Insane as some of these ideas may seem, it's important to recognise where they came from and not to get too caught up in the madness. People have been known to become transfixed by the lunar surface and spend the rest of their lives staring madly into space. That's bad enough when you're talking about the astronomical body; it becomes downright disturbing if you're talking about a poo. Don't let yourself become moonstruck. Face this rune, then flush it away.

---

[70] Statistical evidence, however, exposes this 'well-known fact' as complete bullshit. But who are we to let the truth get in the way of a good story?

🧻 What Action Can I Take?

A lot depends on your reaction to this particular rune. If you looked down between your legs, saw The Moon and thought, 'That looks like a moon. Cool. Hey, that gives me an idea – I'm going to pop down to the hobby store, collect a cardboard tube and a couple of lenses and make my own telescope,' then we don't think you've got anything to worry about. Be careful of paper cuts, and enjoy your holiday project.

If, on the other hand, you looked down between your legs, saw The Moon and thought, 'That looks like a moon. Hey, that reminds me – I promised myself I'd indulge in an orgy of killing and insane violence next time I shat an unusual shape,' you're quite likely beyond help. And we have no desire to be blamed for your inability to tell fantasy from reality; if we wanted to be cited in murder prosecutions we'd design video games, not write books about poo.

Historical Context

This is just too easy. Moon . . . crazy . . . moon . . . crazy . . . Call us crazy, but it's got to be Keith Moon.

Moon was known as one of the wildest men in rock music – and not for nothing. He destroyed his own instruments at the end of gigs and wrecked friends' homes and hotel rooms with equal abandon, on one occasion driving a Cadillac into a hotel swimming pool. He launched television sets through hotel windows and blew up his drum kit on live television, embedding a piece of cymbal in guitarist Pete Townshend's arm, but his party trick – appropriately for a book on botty products – was the destruction of hotel toilets.

It's said that his bog-blasting hobby wreaked over half a million American dollars' worth of damage over his career, and he was banned from several hotel chains for life. Moon had what can only be described as a hate–hate relationship with hotel management. Legend has it that there was one occasion when Moon was asked to turn down his cassette player because the Who were making 'too much noise'. Moon's response was to light a stick of dynamite and drop it down his toilet – apparently to teach the unsuspecting management the difference between the Who and 'too much noise'.

Having, on more than one occasion, looked ruefully at the disgrace in the bowl and thought, 'Bloody hell. I wish I could remove all evidence of *that*', we can only finish by saying: Keith Moon, we salute you.

Inverted

An inverted Moon rune is known in Arsetrological circles as The Sun and indicates a fuzzy, easygoing nature that's a contrast to the shivering mania of the Moon. You might be tempted to think this is an indicator that you're the centre of all things, but don't be confused: just because The Sun came out of your arse, it doesn't mean the sun *shines* out of your arse. Keep your ego in check.

The Beaver

Quick Reading

Build quickly and build well. And don't be crude when you think of beavers – try only to think of wet, furry . . . Oh, what's the point?

 **Rites of Passage**

Calm & Serene

A good, solid dam can provide a stable environment in which to build. Mind you, you'll have some explaining to do to the folks downstream.

Sound & Fury

Oops! Blockage. You may have had the best of intentions, but all you've done is delay the inevitable flood of stagnant water down the river.

 What Did You Eat?

Oh, please. Don't make us say it.

Ignoring the obvious gynaecological references, there are plenty of culinary aspects to The Beaver. For a start, those suckers can bring down entire trees with their ferocious, hillbilly-like teeth. And that's not natural. If you can eat a tree then surely anything that pops up in your bog can have a dietary explanation. And, according to the admittedly rudimentary research undertaken, they also store up sticks and logs under water to feed on during the winter, so maybe we could be a little less concerned about dietary explanations and a little more attentive to splinters.

Detailed Reading

The Beaver is the second-largest rodent in the world (third if you count City traders) and best known for the construction of extremely sophisticated dams and lodges in the river systems of North America and Europe. The Arsetrological significance of this is obvious: the appearance of this rune in your personal dam is a sign that you are ready to begin building your own permanent mark on the landscape. It could be your own home, if you are currently a renter (and, if so, spare a thought for the next tenant and flush vigorously), or it could be a less obvious structure. Have you been toying with the idea of starting your own business? Beginning a family? Blocking off a major tributary or waterway?

If the answer to any of these questions is 'yes', then The Beaver has arrived to tell you that it's time to turn your dream into reality. There may be a few people who say it can't be done, but haters be damned – these buck teeth can make short shrift of any bank manager, contraceptive or coast guard who says nay to your log-based scheme.

What Action Can I Take?

The Beaver says 'build', and build you shall – but beware the many distractions that come with this rune. Beavers are well known for building dams but it should be noted that the reason they build dams is to provide the environment and protection to build a *lodge*. And the lodge is the real home of the beaver.[71] The message is clear: don't become distracted by the first act and forget to follow through to the main event. It's very easy to think that your job is done once you've chewed through the trees, but that's only half the battle.

---

[71] Although the Playboy Mansion runs a close second.

⚏ Historical Context

Beavers are known to be able to rebuild a dam overnight, to be able to block the flow of rivers and to be able to defend themselves, through guile and ingenuity, against what might seem to be stronger predators. If these are the criteria for being the historical beaver – refusal to be beaten, persistence and a willingness to take on and defeat superior forces – then look no further than Boadicea.

Queen of the Brythonic tribe, the Iceni, in the first century, Boadicea rallied her people against the greatest military force the world has ever seen, the Roman Empire, and routed them in Colchester, London and St Albans, before finally being defeated in the Battle of Watling Street. It is thought that she poisoned herself rather than surrender, which was probably a sound move, given that she'd slaughtered more than seventy thousand Romans and the phrase 'ASBO' wouldn't be invented for roughly two thousand years.

Despite the savage nature of her fame, Boadicea could not be faulted for her courage, persistence and willingness to take on a superior foe, so there could be few arguments with the man who was willing to stand up in his local pub and proclaim that Boadicea was the finest beaver in history.

Inverted

From one rodent to another, invert The Beaver and it's pretty clear that the result is The Easter Bunny. This cute, fluffy little purveyor of chocolate goodies is the friend of all small girls and boys – and a stunning example of what happens when you put religious festivals and commercial opportunism into a cultural particle accelerator and smash them together at high speeds. Only that cake-dispensing amphibian, the Yom Kippur Frog, is stranger.

But that's an observation for another time. What concerns us here is that the appearance of The Easter Bunny in your crapper is a sure sign that you need to reassess the contribution you're making to your friends and family. It may seem as if you're making everyone happy with your undeniably welcome yet strangely inappropriate gifts, but, deep down, we think you know you're doing it only to fit in. The Easter Bunny invites you to think again and look for the real spirit of family and friendship.

The Sportsman

Quick Reading

You're dribbling, shooting and pouring on the runs, but the ultimate prize still eludes you.

 **Rites of Passage**

Calm & Serene

You know what you want, it's just a matter of going out and getting it. But first: a crap. And maybe a read of the paper.

Sound & Fury

This bodes ill for you and your atrophied sense of competition. You'd much rather wallow in self-pity than actually put in the hard miles needed to win. That application form you picked up for the SAS? Might as well use the back of it for your shopping list, nancy boy.

What Did You Eat?

If there's a steroid out there that produces shit that shape, you don't want it anywhere near you – no matter how much it increases your performance. A turd like that elbows its way out of your arse with a sound like a frog doing ten minutes on high in an industrial microwave. Probably.

Of course, we know from previous runes that it's not simply a matter of shape in, shape out. If it were, Elvis would have shat hamburgers. No, there are clearly more metaphysical forces at work here. A diet of vitamin supplements, sports drinks and low-fat foods can help your performance, but, ultimately, this is a sign that you're going to have to lift your game. You can start with your wrist muscles – you're going to need to flush three or four times to get this thing down.

Detailed Reading

Some people will say that it doesn't matter whether you win or lose, but it's how you play the game. That, quite frankly, is loser talk. The only one who ever gets a medal for 'trying hard' is the asthmatic nerdy kid with the Coke-bottle glasses. The fact that you *still* haven't won the prize you seek is eating away at you inside.

So what are you going to do about it? Become embittered and take your bat and ball and go home? Or dust yourself off and have another crack at the title? Of course, you may not succeed, but nobody will be able to say you didn't try. So, yes, this is all about the fact that you haven't come to terms with a failure in your past. There's something you always wanted but never attained or – worse still – never had the courage to try. Once you recognise what this might be, you're halfway to the winner's podium.

What Action Can I Take?

What sort of piss-weak, lily-livered, soft-cock question is that? Are you a man or a mouse? Only pretty boys end the game with a clean uniform – time to get down and dirty. At the risk of sounding like a Marine drill sergeant, there is no 'try': there is 'do' or 'fail'! *Now drop and give me twenty!*

Obviously that's a little extreme, but the point is that you have to work if you want this. Anything worth having is worth working for and you, my friend, have been too soft for too long. Time to get out the full-length mirror and have a good hard look at yourself. Train hard, strategise and play for keeps – that's the path to victory and happiness. And, if that doesn't work, fuck it – cheat. Just remember the eleventh commandment: thou shalt not get caught.

ᛗ Historical Context

Obviously there are many famous sporting figures we could choose for this section. But, because we still harbour hopes – however dim – of being invited to the opening ceremony of the next Olympics, we've decided to choose a young man who's been dead for 2,500 years. Legend has it that, at the end of the Battle of Marathon in 490 BCE, Pheidippides ran for twenty-six miles from Marathon to Athens to deliver news of a Greek victory over the Persians, thereby giving us both the name and the distance for the most ridiculous of all Olympic events.

Mind you, another legend has it that Pheidippides ran twenty-six miles from Athens to Sparta to ask for assistance *before* the battle. And this kind of illustrates our point: nobody remembers what Pheidippides actually *did*, but they know he did it *successfully*. Everyone loves a winner.[72]

---

[72] Not that we'd know from personal experience, you understand.

The Sportsman

Inverted

Invert The Sportsman and you arrive, uncannily, at The Zimmer Frame. From the athletic to the infirm, few inversions better capture the essences of the two runes involved. Really. It's incredible. Every now and then, an inverted rune comes along that's so appropriate to the original that we're just about convinced that all this shit may actually have something to it.

The Archangel

Quick Reading

A figure with a halo leads a herd of followers –
but you're not dazzled by his shining ring.

 Rites of Passage

Calm & Serene

This fad will pass and then you alone can rejoice – for
you will be the only one who doesn't need to find a way
to dispose of all those Steps albums without anybody
seeing you.

Sound & Fury

Hanging out with The Man can be fun, but don't you deserve
more than just the crumbs from his table?

What Did You Eat?

Ambrosia? Nectar of the gods? We don't know. What exactly
should you eat to shit out an Archangel? Holy food? You
mean like Swiss cheese or doughnuts?

The fact of the matter is that there is no causal link between
your worldly diet and your heavenly bum fruit. Just accept
it for what it is: a sign from . . . well, not Heaven, exactly, but
from wherever such shitty signs originate, that you, sir, have
been visited by an Archangel. If you don't happen to find
yourself unexpectedly pregnant with the Son of God, then
you can prepare for the imminent presence of some bastard
who thinks he is.

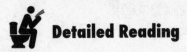 **Detailed Reading**

Some people are just able to get others to follow them – be it through fear, love, respect, an awesome grasp of rhetoric or some bizarre pheromone stink advertised in the back pages of 'gentlemen's periodicals' under the banner 'GET GIRLS FAST!'[73] It seems most of us are natural followers, but a happy few are born to lead. However, the appearance of The Archangel doesn't mean that you're one of those people. Sorry about that.

No, the appearance in your bowl of this arse-angel means that you're going to be one of the sceptical observers sniping from the sidelines. You know the sort – the ones who will watch Beckham stroke home a 30-yard free kick and say, 'No left foot, though.'

Mostly, they're miserable bastards, but they're miserable bastards with a purpose, because the cynical observer has an important role to play in modern life. Most of the people who lead us – whether it's the boss, politicians, religious leaders or even the new manager of your football team – are (and we hope you'll forgive us for getting into advanced arsetrological terminology here) complete wankers. And it's up to you and others like you to provide the voice of reason.

But you do need to exercise some discretion. Sometimes the worst thing you can do to a conman is let him know you're wise to his game. For example, picture the fate of a German in 1942 who said to Hitler, 'Aren't you awfully short and dark for a member of the blond Teutonic master race?'

---

[73] They don't work. Or so, um, a friend told us.

What Action Can I Take?

Many will tell you that you should show some respect for differing opinions – that your own lack of faith doesn't mean you have the right to pooh-pooh someone else's ideas. They are, of course, fucking idiots.

The strategy is pretty clear: there's a new people's hero in town and only you can see him for what he is. Do you calmly explain to his acolytes that he's only human and therefore subject to the same foibles and flaws as the rest of us? Or do you follow him around with a camera until you catch him having a cheeky knee-trembler with the work-experience girl?[74] No doubt about it – get the evidence and stick it on the noticeboard for all to see. Nobody's a leader with his pants around his ankles.

 Historical Context

We're going to have to tread carefully here, because all the obvious candidates for The Archangel are likely to get us in trouble. Pick an actual archangel and you're looking at excommunication (plus, we read in a book that they send a homicidal albino after you). Name a prophet? Fatwa. Even mentioning L. Ron Hubbard will get you a lawsuit *and* a lecture on psychology from a midget with a grin bigger than his own head.

So, rather than start a religious war over a ridiculous toilet book, we're instead going to cite the example of former Aston Villa striker Juan Pablo Angel, who was a record signing at the time and never quite worked out in the way the fans would have liked. We always said he was shit.

---

[74] Of course he will. His kind always does.

Inverted

To be honest, the first thing we thought of when we turned this upside down was 'tits'. But, then, that's the first thing we think of when we see anything,[75] so it didn't seem a particularly sound interpretation. Obviously, the opposite of an angel is a devil and when you're talking about an archangel, the only equivalent is Old Nick himself: Beelzebub, Satan, Dr Naughty or whichever of the many names he's going by these days.[76]

The parallels are clear: just as Satan was exiled from Paradise and into the Underworld, so too was this turd exiled from *your* magic kingdom and cast down below. (That's why there's no standard rune called The Devil, because inverting *that* would mean an ascent of a most uncomfortable nature, the likes of which are occasionally seen when the cabin pressure goes wrong in an aeroplane toilet.) Either way, it's an object lesson in what can happen when you point out somebody's flaws. And you thought getting chucked out of the pub was bad . . .

---

[75] Except, oddly enough, tits: they make us think of football.
[76] I'm pretty sure 'Dr Naughty' isn't one of them. – Ed.

The Au Pair

Quick Reading

Someone else has dropped a load in your lap and now you're left holding the baby. Unsurprisingly, the little tyke needs changing and you're all out of nappies.

 Rites of Passage

Calm & Serene

If you approach this with the right attitude, you could turn a problem into an opportunity. Yup, we're going to try to shag the babysitter.[77]

Sound & Fury

You're feeling resentful, which is understandable, but nobody else is going to clean up after you. Leave *that* in the bowl for too long and it's only a matter of time before the neighbours complain about the smell. Again.

What Did You Eat?

Given that many au pairs come from Scandinavia, is it possible that you've been snacking on one too many of the girlfriend's Ryvitas? The combination of rustic crackerbreads, hot saunas and repeat plays of *Abba: Gold* may lead to the formation of The Au Pair, but are just as likely to result in your coming out of the closet and heading off for a *fabulous* night at the local moustache club, if you get our meaning.

---

[77] This is, of course, dependent on your babysitter being of legal age for that sort of thing *and* your wife/girlfriend not finding out. And, if this is your significant other reading this overly long footnote, it's just a joke, all right, love? You can't blame him for what *we're* thinking.

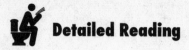

Detailed Reading

An arrangement that was once mutually satisfying has turned sour. Whether this partnership started as friendship or purely business, it has now turned into something rather unsavoury. This is best demonstrated by the unpleasant mess that's been handed to you without any sort of warning. The problem wasn't of your making, but there's nobody else who's going to deal with it. Or – even worse – the problem was *entirely* of your making, but you'd managed to convince yourself that you could get somebody else to clean it up.

This rune can be applied to all walks of life. It could refer to a once-promising business partnership that has ended in acrimony, or it could be a much more personal situation – like the time one of us (we're not telling you which) threw up all over his girlfriend's bathroom[78] and then couldn't understand why she made *him* clean it up. He was quite sure that, having relieved himself of eight pints of lager and a doner kebab, he could crawl gratefully into bed and sleep until ACDC stopped playing a gig inside his head, but somehow it wasn't to be. If only he'd had The Au Pair to warn him of this possibility, he'd have stuck his fingers down his throat while he was still in the front garden.

We seem to have got off the point, which is that The Au Pair signals an unpleasant task, but one that needs to be done. It may not be fair, it may not be right, but it's up to you to do it.

---

[78] Technically, it wasn't *all over* the bathroom – he cunningly managed to miss the toilet bowl.

What Action Can I Take?

Well, we don't want to belabour the point here, but it seems to us that the central theme of The Au Pair thus far has been that, no matter how unfair or unappealing you may deem the situation in which you find yourself, the only rational solution is for you to *clean this mess up*!

Jesus, what the fuck is *wrong* with you? We can't make it any clearer. *You* have to do this or it won't get done. Medieval kings may have had personal assistants to help them wipe their arses but you, my friend, have to do your own paperwork.

 Historical Context

We racked our brains for a long time over this one, but – and we know this will surprise you – there are very few famous au pairs in the history books. None, in fact. So we tried babysitters. Still no luck. The only thing left was to explore historical instances of someone being left a God-awful mess to tidy up. You know, like, say, a president of a really powerful nation spends his two terms (for argument's sake) in office squandering whatever good will his country has built up; launching illegal and unwinnable wars against the wrong enemy; fucking over the country's constitution by showing no respect for due process or, indeed, the law; illegally imprisoning his enemies; kicking back lucrative government contracts to his corporate cronies, most of whom are incompetent or downright evil; and then walking out when his term is finished, leaving some other poor sap to clean up the mess.

But we couldn't think of anyone like that. Any ideas?

Inverted

In this age of political correctness, we're reluctant to draw specific conclusions from this, but when you invert The Au Pair you get The Testicle. We're not saying there's any relevance to this beyond the sad, middle-aged fantasies of a few desperate men[79] – we're just stating the facts.

The Testicle, as we're sure everyone is aware, has a twofold significance. First, it is a sign of great potency – from testicles' biological, life-giving nature to their use as a metaphor for a man's courage. But The Testicle is also, paradoxically, a man's greatest weakness – metaphorically, referring to extreme (and sometimes unwarranted) pride, but also to the undeniable defeat that inevitably follows a swift kick being delivered to them.

What does this mean in Arsetrological terms? Simply this: be aware that your greatest strength may also be your greatest weakness. Exercise it with care.

[79] A 'few'? Or 'two'? – Ed

The Minstrel

Quick Reading

There's a song in the air! And something that
sounds a little like a trumpet.

 ## Rites of Passage

Calm & Serene

Given the gentle, folk-rock way this tune is playing, perhaps
it's time to take out the old guitar and have a quick strum.

Sound & Fury

The anal power chords are ripping and shredding, creating an
ungodly racket that bangs your head on the toilet wall.

What Did You Eat?

They say that music may be the food of love, but that's
putting things in reverse and we're not sure quite how one
goes about actually eating love, so we'll stop on this line of
thinking before we create a paradox and disappear up our
own arseholes. In which case, we're looking at an unusually
shaped stool that suggests the unhealthy snacking that
comes from life on the road. Time to cut down on the lager
breakfasts and the kebab-and-cocaine lunches.

 **Detailed Reading**

Even if you're usually a tone deaf monkey with less musical ability than a professional footballer's girlfriend, the appearance of The Minstrel in your toilet bowl shows that — for a time, at least — you will have the heart and soul of an artiste.

None of the talent, however, so you're going to be an insufferable prick for the foreseeable future — vain, arrogant and with no discernible skill to back up your overdeveloped ego. But, while you remain a talentless baboon, you project an aura of stardom that belies your utter lack of ability. This doesn't mean that you're going to headline Glastonbury, but it might mean you get a few pairs of knickers flung your way. Sure, some of them might be soiled, but your overdeveloped ego should be able to cope with that. Enjoy the attention while it lasts, because your time in the spotlight will be short.

But how do you go back to a regular life once your star power has waned? Do you bow out gracefully, or desperately try to claw your way back into the limelight? Sadly, once you've had a slice of success, it's difficult to go back to normality. Many a Minstrel has taken the quest for fame too far and wound up humiliating themselves in the nightclubs, holiday camps and cruise ships of the world. Show a little decorum and get off the stage, before you become a public laughing stock.

What Action Can I Take?

Of course, you could use this as the catalyst for actually learning an instrument, but to your lazy ears this will sound too much like hard work, so it's more likely that you'll pursue the sex and drugs without actually bothering with the rock and roll. This is a path that worked for Sid Vicious and Pete Doherty, so perhaps there's something in it. On the other hand, given how those two fellas ended up, perhaps you'd be better off staying at home and practising the banjo.

 ## Historical Context

In that special place where shite and genius meet, it couldn't be anyone else but the Austrian prodigy Johann Chrysostom Wolfgang Amadeus Mozart, a man with even more talent than he had names. Born in January 1756 and dying in December 1791, Mozart filled his not-quite-thirty-six years with an enormous body of work of the highest order. He produced more than six hundred pieces, many of which rank among the finest in the history of classical music.

Viewers of the 1984 film *Amadeus* will be familiar with Mozart's foibles, eccentricities and fondness for scatological humour. Amazingly, for an industry so utterly devoid of respect for the truth, it seems that Hollywood got Mozart's character pretty spot-on. He was, indeed, obsessed with the botty and all its products, and even went so far as to write a canon called *Leck Mich im Arsch*, which translates literally as 'lick me in the arse'. Genius, indeed.

The Minstrel

Inverted

An inverted minstrel is self-effacing and modest and shies away from the spotlight. Unlike the empty sound and fury of the regular rune, it's likely to signify some actual talent and therefore has absolutely nothing to do with the modern music industry. Much as we'd like to propose that such a description fits writers such as ourselves, you and we know this isn't true. So the inverted Minstrel is, in fact, The Roadie – there to support the artist, lug their equipment and drink their beer.

The Alchemist

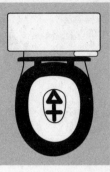

Quick Reading

Presumably you've heard of King Midas, who turned anything he touched to gold. Well, you appear to have the opposite power . . .

 Rites of Passage

Calm & Serene

One man's crap is another man's compost. All you need do is find a way to turn seemingly catastrophic events to your advantage.

Sound & Fury

On the other hand, you can't make strawberry jam out of shit.

What Did You Eat?

Just as alchemists strive to turn lead into gold, your digestive tract is struggling to transform all that protein, carbohydrates, roughage, green vegetables, omega-3 into . . . well, jobbies. Given that this rune has certain physical features that would seem to defy physical possibility, we'd suggest that, if you've managed to pass an Alchemist without bleeding to death, then whatever you're eating must have remarkable healing powers.

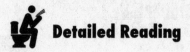

Detailed Reading

In ancient times, men would dedicate their lives to the mystic art of alchemy, hoping one day to discover how to turn base metals into gold. Alchemists spent their lives working to discover the secret of transmutation or searching for the Philosopher's Stone. Not one of them succeeded. But, in case you're tempted to feel sorry for the poor saps, consider this: none of this would have been necessary if this bunch of loonies had taken half the time they spent on their fruitless quest and used it mining. You know – for gold.

This is important because, in Arsetrological terms, gold is the opposite of shit. And what does all this mean? Basically, that everything you touch turns to crap. Whether it's your own plans or those of a friend, your role is to stagger around, knocking things over and staining the carpet. You, my friend, are the spanner in the works, the fly in the ointment, the peanut in the poo.

This isn't a conscious choice on your part and the process appears quite involuntary, but that's cold comfort[80] to the people whose lives you're ruining. Unsurprisingly, they're quite browned off, but your transformative powers work only one way, so there's no hope of turning their frowns upside down.

---

[80] Or possibly warm, steaming comfort.

⊙ What Action Can I Take?

Luckily, you don't need to know anything about chemistry, magic or secret incantations to affect a transmutation, as the magic is already stored in your mighty ring of power. You might even say you can do this stuff sitting down, but how does one cope with such an unfortunate affliction? It may seem that hiding yourself away from the world is your only option, but that's a short-term solution at best. Sooner or later you'll need to come up for air.

Instead, you have to learn how to make the best of your lot. Believe it or not, there are some viable markets for shite – organic gardeners need fertiliser, Channel 4 needs programme ideas and certain specialist publications pay good rates for pictures taken through a glass-topped coffee table.

⚜ Historical Context

If it's alchemy you seek, good reader, why look no further than the sixteenth-century astronomer, astrologer, mathematician, occultist, adviser to Queen Elizabeth I – and, of course, alchemist – Doctor John Dee.

Dee's work was in equal parts sorcery and science – much as the runes in this book are equal parts prophecy and bloody good shit. Difficult though we might find it to believe, today, that anyone in a position of power or privilege could let themselves be influenced by superstition, Dee spent much of his life trying to work out how to talk to angels,[81] who he believed could teach him the universal language of creation.

John Dee advised and tutored Elizabeth I as well as a

---

[81] Trying unsuccessfully, as it happens. We don't know about you, but a few Valium and half a bottle of Scotch usually does the trick for us, talking-to-angels-wise.

number of her court, notably Elizabeth's spymaster, Francis Walsingham, and William Cecil, the Lord High Treasurer. The repercussions of these relationships are still being felt today – how else to explain the fact that the British intelligence services are intent on climbing up our arses with a microscope and the economy's in the shit?

Inverted

After all our talk of mythological kings and Elizabethan sorcerers, it seems a little prosaic to point out that, when you invert The Alchemist, you get The Shovel. It is, however, very appropriate – and not just because you have to shift the crap with something. The correct interpretation of The Alchemist calls for the full acceptance of the problem at hand, and a genuine attempt to resolve it.

But, if your turd tumbled into the bowl upside down, you have another option – one that may be too seductive to resist. So everything you've touched has turned to shit and you're wondering what to do about it? While everyone around you is exhorting you to clean it up, there is another option open to a recipient of an inverted rune: bury it.

Sure, that's avoiding rather than solving the problem. Sure, that's a quick fix, at best, and won't actually make the problem go away. *But* . . . it should give you time to get your affairs in order and get out of town. Then it's somebody else's problem. In the meantime, just think of what it'll do for your tomato plants . . .

The Atom

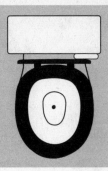

Quick Reading

Good things come in small packages. But they really shouldn't hurt so much to produce.

Rites of Passage

Calm & Serene

Size isn't everything. It's possible to contain immense potential in an unimposing form.

Sound & Fury

It's small only because it hasn't exploded yet. Like a wet fart, this is the signal that a scene of enormous devastation is on its way.

What Did You Eat?

Not much, by the looks of things. Enjoy feasting on that single pea, did you?

In many ways, this is the most difficult rune to decipher from a dietary perspective. It doesn't matter what you ate, because none of it has come out, anyway. The Arsetrological implications of this are quite straightforward: interpret The Atom as a genuine predictive event, as there can be no outside stimuli.

Presumably, there are foods that cause the arsehole to slam shut like the airlock on a submarine, but the odds are good that you haven't eaten them – they're in very short supply in the developed world, as most of them are snapped up by altar boys and first-year students at public school.

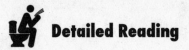

Detailed Reading

Obviously, the diminutive size of The Atom indicates there are certain physiological issues pressing upon you at the moment. Whether due to stress, ill health or perhaps even financial pressures,[82] you're finding it extremely hard to relax – even sitting down doesn't seem to help. This results in one of the most pathetic Arsetrological runes in the pantheon.

But don't let the small size of The Atom deceive you. Powerful forces are contained within its tiny shell, although unlocking its potential is a process that contains many dangerous possibilities. Thanks to advances in plumbing, the risk of a chain reaction is greatly reduced, but you should still treat this little peanut of plop with respect. While it seems unimaginable that something so small could contain the power to change your world, it's worth remembering what splitting the atom did to the twentieth century. The manifestation of this rune indicates that radical change is possible, but will take hard work to accomplish. And you should definitely be careful of fallout.

While working your way though this rune, do bear in mind that there's no such thing as a partially split atom – you either stay whole or explode with unimaginable energy. There are no half-measures and you need to weigh the potential consequences with utmost gravity. Perhaps this mnemonic rhyme will help:

> *Tensely clench,*
> *uncomfortable dance.*
> *Dare to relax,*
> *destroy your pants.*

We think there's something in there for all of us.

---

[82] Where did you think the term 'tight arse' came from?

What Action Can I Take?

Mighty oaks from tiny acorns grow. This rune is a clear sign that there is an event of immense potential waiting to spring forth. Whether it grows like a mighty oak, to be a source of strength and beauty for all around you, or explodes like a mushroom cloud of shit and partially digested curry is really up to you.

You need to search deep inside yourself[83] to discover whether your imminent event is malignant or benign. If you find nothing but corruption, you'll need a controlled explosion to resolve the issue. We'd suggest colonic irrigation or a good dose of salts and nice sit-down. If you feel that the potential waiting to be released is a force for good – and, we must say, we think this unlikely, on balance – then it is up to you to nurture it into maturity.[84]

Historical Context

There are a number of candidates for this but, after much thought, we decided that the most appropriate figure was the man known as 'the father of the atomic bomb', J. Robert Oppenheimer.

As the scientific director of the Manhattan Project, Oppenheimer might be expected to have been a firm advocate of the use of atomic weapons, but this is far from the truth. As he watched the Trinity test in New Mexico, the final test before the bomb would be deployed against the cities of Hiroshima and Nagasaki, he famously recalled the words of Krishna from the Bhagavad Gita: 'Now I am become Death, the destroyer of worlds.'

---

[83] You may find a mirror and a speculum helpful for this.
[84] This word is probably unknown to you. Look it up in a dictionary.

The relevance of this should be obvious to those who have taken the path of the laxative in an attempt to explore the potential of The Atom. After the inevitable botty blast, with your ringpiece in tatters and the last echo of the explosion finally fading, well may you look down between your legs and remember Oppenheimer's famous words. And, once you've done that, get yourself to a doctor before you bleed to death.

Inverted

There is no 'up' in quantum physics – this is still The Atom, no matter which way you look at it.

The Lovers

Quick Reading

Find contentment with one who understands you
and your ways. As the poets say, 'Love me, love
my shit.'

 Rites of Passage

Calm & Serene

By accepting and acting on this rune, you are certain to find
true inner peace, contentment and all the other bullshit
you're looking for in a fortune-telling book.

Sound & Fury

Your search for the yin to complement your yang can lead to
relationships of an addictive or parasitic nature. Watch out
for worms!

What Did You Eat?

An excellent question. If music be the food of love, as
Shakespeare suggests, then it seems somebody's been
playing a few bum notes. Of course, there are many
foodstuffs associated with the physical act of love[85] –
oysters, figs, chocolate, Spanish fly, horny goat weed,
asparagus – and it's possible that any of them may have
contributed to the formation of The Lovers in your toilet
bowl. Mind you, there are also a lot of foods that look like a
cock,[86] and we shouldn't, in all good conscience, forget them:
hot dogs, bananas, sausages, corn on the cob – any or all

---

[85] That's a surprisingly coy turn of phrase for you guys. – Ed.
[86] Ah. And the status quo is restored . . . – Ed.

of these foods, coupled with the appearance of The Lovers, could well be sufficient to help you put your toad in the hole. And you can't really ask for more than that, can you?

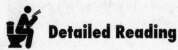 **Detailed Reading**

Despite what you may think, The Lovers isn't necessarily about romantic relationships (although obviously it's not a bad harbinger for such things). Instead, the rune indicates that there's someone or something out there that fully complements you and is the key to your future happiness.

This could be as simple as finding somebody who likes the soft chocolates while you like the hard ones, or it could be as pathetic as learning that the local bar has a half-price-pint evening every month on the exact day you get paid. It could even be the mythical nymphomaniac girlfriend whose father owns a pub and who turns into a pizza at midnight (thereby leading to an embarrassing trip to the burns ward if you don't get your timing right). A man can dream.

However, while this missing piece is usually manifested in the form of a person, it isn't necessarily so. Sometimes it's something as simple as an idea. What it definitely *isn't* however, is a new car or expensive piece of technology. The Lovers is a call for you to transcend material possessions and get in touch with your heart. Or, failing that, your knob.

What Action Can I Take?

Unlike with most of the runes contained in this book, there's very little downside to The Lovers. All you require is the will and the courage to assess your life honestly and decide what it is that's missing. Your task, if you are to make full use of The Lovers, is to seek out that which can make you whole. Unless you can find it you are destined to be unfulfilled; but, if you succeed, you will be so much more than the sum of your parts. Probably. Don't quote us or anything. Our idea of Nirvana is to snap one off so cleanly that we don't need to wipe our arse, so we're hardly authorities on universal happiness.

Historical Context

There are many examples of couples throughout history who have become inseparable in the popular imagination – Humphrey Bogart and Lauren Bacall; Elizabeth Taylor and Richard Burton; Salman Rushdie and a bloody good hiding place – but, as has become custom, we decided to choose the ones most likely to provide a cheap laugh at their expense.

Thus, we explore Mark Antony and Cleopatra. Clearly, this famous pair of lovers could well have done with a pair of *soixante-neuf*-shaped turds floating in their bowl, to help them make the best of their tumultuous relationship. While it's obvious that both Antony and Cleopatra were infatuated with each other, there's no evidence that the attraction went any deeper than the purely physical, whereas the nature of The Lovers is that the person, place or thing that fully complements you operates at a much more fundamental level.

The Lovers

Despite the dramatic manner in which Cleopatra killed herself following Antony's death, their relationship seemed to be predominantly sexual, thereby illustrating that, even with the great tragic figures of romance, it all comes down to tits and asp in the end.

Inverted

Obviously, there is no topological difference between The Lovers and The Lovers Inverted. Metaphorically, you could say the opposite of The Lovers is The Enemies, but we fail to see how you could possibly tell the difference. It's very much a case of 'same shit, different shovel'.

You could, if you wish, say that there is a fundamental sense of competition and even enmity that is an essential part of the lovemaking process as you both bid to provide and receive pleasure at the same time – your base instinct being driven by the electrochemical signals your engorged genitals are sending to your brain, even while that part of you that rides above the animal sensations is engaged in as selfless an act of giving pleasure as it can – and that fundamental dichotomy is nowhere better expressed than in the very circular act of the sixty-nine position.

You *could* say that, but frankly it's a bit of a mouthful.

The Rabbit Warren

Quick Reading

At the end of a dark passage lurks a terrible beast, and, no matter how distasteful it may be, you'll have to face it in the end.

Rites of Passage

Calm & Serene

You may think avoidance is the best strategy, but stand up for yourself. You've got to be a man and unleash the beast.

Sound & Fury

Rabbit droppings are small and easily overlooked in the dark. When you're tiptoeing through the place where hundreds of rabbits are living, resign yourself to the fact your shoes are going to get dirty.

What Did You Eat?

Rabbits, of course, are always on a diet. How else to explain their constant menu of lettuce, carrots and low-fat cottage cheese? But can that lead to the crippling fear described below? Probably not. Eat nothing but rabbit food for too long and you'll be too weak to feel fear. You know what you need to build your strength up? A nice rabbit stew – full of protein. *Watership Down*: you've read the book, you've seen the film, now . . . try the stew!

Detailed Reading

You're in a dark, dark place with no idea which way to turn. How you got there is irrelevant. What matters is how you get out. Unfortunately, all roads lead to the same place – the heart of the labyrinth.

And here lies the beast – a creature with burning red eyes and huge teeth. You hear its sounds echoing off the walls and your heart quickens with terror. Much as you don't want to enter the beast's lair, the maze of tunnels offers you no choice. So you step into the chamber, resigned to the fact that you'll be torn limb from limb by whatever foul creature lurks within, but determined to meet your fate with head held high and bowels unvoided.

Imagine your surprise, then, when you see that the 'beast' in question is, in fact, a fluffy bunny rabbit. Don't feel foolish, though – the important thing is that you confronted your fear and can walk away with your head held high. At least, until you have to explain the state of your underpants . . .

What Action Can I Take?

The Rabbit Warren calls for a strategy that is, at the same time, the most straightforward and the most difficult. To extricate yourself from this maze, you need the courage to walk forward into the dark and face your fear.

The nature of fear is that the threat is always far worse than the reality. As Franklin D. Roosevelt famously said in his first inauguration speech, 'the only thing we have to fear is fear itself . . .' Mind you, since he said that in the midst of the Great Depression and a scant half-dozen years before Hitler's tanks rolled into Poland and plunged the world into the bloodiest war of all time, it's not entirely unfair to level the charge that he was, in fact, talking shit.

Be that as it may – and we'll leave it to people far more boring than we are, to debate the finer points of presidential rhetoric – the point is that you must gird up your loins,[87] screw your courage to the sticking place[88] and meet your fear head on. And, if your fear *does* actually turn out to be a force of horrifying power and violence, as opposed to the small, fluffy bunny you were promised above, we can only apologise and direct your attention to the disclaimer at the beginning of this book.[89]

 **Historical Context**

Caught in a maze and can't find your way out? Certain beyond all shadow of a doubt that something terrible lurks on the heart of the labyrinth? You could do worse than learn from the tale of Theseus.

In Greek mythology, Theseus was a legendary king of Athens and son of either King Aegeus or the god Poseidon.[90] After many heroic deeds (which, quite frankly, lack the comic potential of fighting a half-man-half-bull, and so will remain untold here), he found himself part of a regular tribute of young boys and girls that Athens was obliged to pay King Minos of Crete. It was the fate of these youths to be driven into the labyrinth and devoured by the Minotaur (we're sure you've been on package holidays just like it).

Theseus, however, had two advantages the monster's previous victims did not: the love of the king's daughter,

---

[87] The Bible's way of saying 'don't shit yourself'.

[88] Shakespeare's way of saying 'don't shit yourself'.

[89] And, of course, point out that you are now free to shit yourself.

[90] The results of the paternity test aren't in yet, but our money's on Poseidon. Those ancient gods just couldn't keep it in their pants.

Ariadne, who gave him a ball of wool with which to knit a sweater if he became cold[91]; and a sword, which he'd secreted in his tunic. Theseus came upon the Minotaur and slew it after a mighty battle. He then followed the wool trail he'd left back out of the labyrinth and left Crete with Ariadne and the surviving Athenians.

The historical lesson is clear. To defeat even the most fearsome foe, you need to face it bravely and head-on. Also, it doesn't hurt to cheat like a bastard.

Inverted

Tricky. As The Rabbit Warren is a collection of dots, it's tempting to argue that there's no difference between its normal state and inversion. This, however, would be rational and sensible and therefore entirely out of keeping with the spiritual nature of this tome. Therefore, we're going to declare that this random collection of dots is, in fact, representative of The Cosmos. Where the Rabbit Warren is all dark and subterranean, its inverted state is all about space and celestial navigation. There's no enemy here and in space, no one can hear you shit.

---

[91] Or, in the more accepted version of the myth, to unwind as he entered the maze, thereby showing him the way out. I know research can be hard work, but thirty seconds on the internet could have sorted this one out guys – Ed.

The Walking Stick

Quick Reading

You may appear old and crusty, but there's no flies on you. Yet.

Rites of Passage

Calm & Serene

Despite its fearsome shape, this one has slipped out nice and easy, allowing you to relax and enjoy the wisdom that comes with age.

Sound & Fury

No wonder you're grumpy if you're shitting out turds with butchers' hooks on the end – all the better to snag the last turkey in the shop.

What Did You Eat?

You know time's marching on when the first course of every meal you eat is vitamins. But, be that as it may, no dietary supplement known to medical science can explain the insanely shaped shit currently sunning itself in your bog.

If the appearance of The Walking Stick is your first indication that Father Time is lurking round the corner holding a club with your name on it, the odds are that you've yet to make the sorts of compromise in your diet that make our autumn years so much fun. And by 'fun' we do, of course, mean 'living hell'. 'What Did You Eat?' is not really the question any longer: it's been replaced by 'What Can I Eat Without Having to Call for the Nurse?' The answer to which is: not much, sorry.

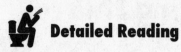

Detailed Reading

It may feel as if you've jumped straight from hip to hip replacement, but you need to put things into perspective. There are advantages to a more mature outlook and you're able calmly to assess situations that would panic younger heads than yours. Like looking into the bowl and seeing bits of your prostate gland mixed in with last night's dinner.[92]

One of the benefits of getting older is that you don't feel the need to impress people quite so much. You're comfortable in your own skin and have enough perspective to realise what's really important. The downside, of course, is that you're missing a little bit of that youthful vitality. Experience and wisdom are great things, but they don't compensate for the fact that your pubes are going grey and you can't drink more than two pints without falling asleep. Quite frankly, if the price for inner peace is losing your hair, low tolerance for spicy foods, incontinence and erectile dysfunction, we think we prefer youthful insecurity, if it's all the same to you.

But that's the whole point of The Walking Stick. You are getting old – that much is irrefutable. It's how you deal with it that's the issue here.

What Action Can I Take?

When you've got hold of a walking stick you really have only two options: use it as a crutch to keep yourself upright and mobile, or spin it round, grab the wrong end and use the handle to beat the shit out of people. Same choice here.

---

[92] A friend who studied nursing told us the bits of prostate look uncannily like the onion in French onion soup – a dish for which we find we've lost all appetite.

The way you respond to The Walking Stick very much depends on how you view the message it has for you. If you're willing to accept that, fair enough, you're not getting any younger, you can look upon The Walking Stick as a badge of honour. You've earned this experience, dammit, and in the right hands such a prop can add quite the air of sophistication.

If, however, you prefer the Dylan Thomas approach and intend to rage, rage against the dying of the light, then you'd be well advised to ready your best crotchety catchphrases and prepare to make the lives of all around you a living nightmare. Here are a few grumpy-old-man sayings to start you off:

- 'That's not music: it's just noise';
- 'It was all fields round here when I was a lad';
- 'If that ball comes over my fence one more time, I'll burst it';
- 'Ah, bugger! I've shit myself again. Nurse!'

🏛 Historical Context

Although history is replete with examples of people who lived to a ripe old age and matured like a fine wine, becoming better as they grew older, there is one name that has become a byword for long life: Methuselah.

According to most versions of the Bible, Methuselah was the grandfather of Noah. He lived to be 969 years old – according to Genesis 5:27: 'And all the days of Methuselah were nine hundred sixty and nine years: and he died.' While even the most fervent biblical scholar will accept a certain allegorical status to this claim, it's worth considering one pertinent question: if you *did* live to be 969 years old, what would you do with all that time?

Bearing in mind that these ancient times didn't have *Countdown*, Viagra or chain-pub Liver-and-Bacon Pensioners' Specials, we're compelled to wonder what Methuselah did for all those years. Probably went slowly gaga, which might account for a few of the more outlandish passages in the Bible. (Seriously, have you ever read that thing? It's got some of the craziest shit you've ever heard — eunuchs, talking donkeys and God mooning Moses. It really does make the *Sunday Sport* look like Pulitzer Prize-winning journalism.)

Inverted

Is it fate or is it intervention by the god of fashion accessorising that inverts The Walking Stick and gives you The Coat Hook? And the interpretations of the two runes are very similar but The Coat Hook is, perhaps counterintuitively, even more extreme.

Consider the positive interpretation: a gentleman of standing and reputation enters an exclusive club or restaurant, and what's the first thing that's said to him after he's greeted? 'May I take your coat, sir?' The clear implication is that, if you accept and embrace The Coat Hook, you can parlay the rune into a lasting respect for your experience and wisdom.

Conversely, what is the abiding image of the grumpy old man? Yes, it's the pervert in the stained overcoat, pulling it open to expose himself to the unwary, crying out, 'Yaaahh! Copaloadathatyabastards! *Yaaaaaahh!*'

The Python

Quick Reading

This enormous serpent is squeezing the life out of you. It's becoming very difficult to breathe – but, given what's lurking below, do you really want to?

 Rites of Passage

Calm & Serene

You are cosy and warm in the embrace of— No, this is horrible. Shed your skin and make good your escape.

Sound & Fury

Well, you were tempted by the python's power but now you realise that you can't breathe and you're covered in shite.

What Did You Eat?

While it may feel as if the only way you could possibly have produced this gargantuan turd is by swallowing an entire fire hose, it's perhaps worth looking at some more sensible suggestions. A Cumberland sausage, perhaps, or maybe a liquorice whirl or two? While snakes are eaten by some brave souls, we're assuming your diet is a little more pedestrian. You don't eat snakes – *or do you*? Because, if the health inspectors are to be believed, all sorts of shit goes into a meat processor – from rat droppings to horse lips, so who's to say a couple of pythons haven't slipped into the grinder? It might account for the humungous, unbroken nature of this particular rune.

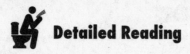 **Detailed Reading**

Caught in the coils of a seemingly inescapable situation, you're desperately struggling to catch your breath. This is the effect of The Python – you've been bewitched into the embrace of a smooth-talking serpent.

Like the snake in the Garden of Eden, The Python first appears friendly, and offers something you didn't even know you wanted. You thought you'd go along with it for a while – after all, you can walk away at any time, right? Wrong. The sneaky snake's mellifluous tones persuaded you to come closer . . . closer . . . and before you knew it you were tangled in his clutches.

This is a sign that a situation or relationship you once thought of as warm and secure has become constrictive and stifling. It could be the job that you're no longer excited about, the hobby you find has lost its allure or the girlfriend who's finally let you take her up the poo chute and is, therefore, not quite the princess you thought she was. Whatever the situation, just struggling against the tangled embrace will only make things worse. Instead, you might be better off using The Python's tactics against him. Try a bit of smooth talking yourself and the two of you might be able to come to some sort of understanding.[93]

---

[93] This is especially worth pursuing with your, ahem, accommodating girlfriend.

What Action Can I Take?

It's difficult to tell a snake's head from its tail, so be careful how you handle things. In fact, if you're the sort to take advice like this overly literally, don't handle things at all. The slippery, smothering embrace of The Python is nothing compared with the suffocating disgust sure to be directed at you should you be discovered with a three-foot length of shite in your hands.

Your first course of action must be – and we can't believe you need to be told this – to flush the toilet. Probably more than once. Ever tried to kill a real snake? Little fuckers take forever to go down.

Once you've cleared the decks, much of The Python's hypnotic attraction will be gone – poor bugger – and you can set about determining whether or not you really need everything the slippery fellow has talked you into.

 Historical Context

It didn't take us long to come to a decision on the best historical exemplar of The Python. We're talking about the original dodgy salesman who offers you the world, the Serpent from the Garden of Eden. While there have been many great con jobs perpetrated since, none has quite matched up to that very first hornswoggle. Scamming a granny out of her nest egg by claiming she needs the guttering radiation-proofed is nothing to the swindling of innocence perpetrated by the original huckster. That forked-tongued bastard has a lot to answer for.

The Python

The Python

Inverted

This is a very clear case of thematic opposites, such as rarely occurs in the Arsetrological world. For every characteristic of The Python, the opposite is true of its inverted form, The Cobra. The Python kills by constriction, The Cobra by venom. The python is large and cumbersome, The Cobra lithe and swift. The Python seizes its prey by slowly coiling around it, and The Cobra attacks by rapidly uncoiling and using the resulting momentum to strike out at its prey. And remember: The Cobra spits venom – so always use thoroughly absorbent paper.

The Bear

Quick Reading

Lurking in the bowl is a huge brown beast. Hiding will do you no good – it has your scent.

 ## Rites of Passage

Calm & Serene

Whatever you're running from, it isn't worth it. Slow down and make peace with the beast that pursues you.

Sound & Fury

Bad news. The beast doesn't want an apology: it wants your arse. And you'd better hope that's a figure of speech . . .

What Did You Eat?

Bears are known to have several culinary weaknesses – most famous among them are a fondness for fish, honey and pic-a-nic baskets.

The fact of the matter is there's no real help to be had in studying your diet. The Bear is coming for you. You *will* shit yourself. The Bear will smell it and it *will* find you. The best you can do is to eat something with lots of cashews in it – hey, it *might* slow down to pick out some nutty morsels.

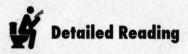 Detailed Reading

You may think that you're smarter than the average bear, but that won't make a difference when you're confronted with the razor-sharp claws of this huge predator.

For some reason The Bear is after you and these fearsome creatures can track their prey for miles. This is due in no small part to their amazing sense of smell. With this in mind, you need to clean yourself up. While it's perfectly understandable – natural, even – to soil yourself in the face of such a threat, if you are to survive The Bear, you must remember two things:

1. a human being can't outrun a bear – but, then again, you don't have to, because . . .
2. if you can smear enough shit on somebody else,[94] maybe the beast will hunt them, instead.

Alternatively, for those with a more moralistic view,[95] perhaps it's time to take stock and wash away the sins of old. You see, The Bear represents your own fears. Make amends for your past misdeeds and you'll buy yourself some time. But that won't fool The Bear for long. Your fears can be concealed for only a short time and eventually you must confront them. After all, what's the worst that could happen?

---

[94] Preferably someone slower than you.
[95] And a casual disregard for their own safety.

What Action Can I Take?

To be honest, we're having a hard time coming up with a better strategy than the shit-smearing tactic above, but if we really must . . .

Popular methods for dealing with bears include a sharp punch on the nose, lying down and playing dead, and bribery. Let's look at them in more detail, shall we? The punch on the nose – as recommended by Stig 'Lefty' McAwber, author of the-less-than successful books *Bear-Taunting for Beginners: 101 Uses for a Prosthetic Hand* and *My Iron Lung and Me: A User's Guide.*

Enough said?

Lying down and playing dead – recommended by . . . well, nobody, as it happens. There's a zero survival rate on this one. Shall we move on?

That just leaves bribery, and that's not as daft as it seems. Bears do have a sweet tooth, but they can't be bribed with chocolate. Well, they probably can, but we seriously doubt you've got access to that much of the brown stuff. *That* brown stuff, anyway.

Nope, nope and nope. All things considered, we're in favour of dumping your shit on somebody else and running like fuck.

 # Historical Context

If The Bear represents your fears, who better to encapsulate the rune than the man who tamed this wild beast for all generations to follow. We speak of none other than the twenty-sixth President of the United States of America, Theodore 'Teddy' Roosevelt.

Roosevelt was a true polymath: hunter, naturalist, historian, explorer, author, soldier and originator of the saying 'Speak softly and carry a big stick.'[96] The youngest man ever to become president, Teddy was leader of the Republican Party, but his distrust of wealthy businessmen, promotion of universal healthcare and conservation of resources would have made him as welcome in the modern party as . . . well as a softly spoken man waving a stick covered in shit.

Lest we be accused of wandering off the topic, while on a hunting trip in 1902, Roosevelt was the only member of the party who hadn't made a kill. A number of his cronies chased down a black bear cub, beat it insensible and tied it to a tree. They then invited Roosevelt to shoot it, but he famously refused to do so, and so was born the legend of 'Teddy's bear'.[97]

Inverted

The inverted Bear looks suspiciously like a hand to us. But what can that mean? Very few texts are able to shed light on this configuration because The Hand is an extremely modern rune. It derives from the I-don't-want-to-hear-it attitude so prevalent in ~~little shits~~ young people today, and is a sign that, although your fears may be pursuing you (as per the reading of The Bear), you don't have to take crap like that. Talk to The Hand because the face ain't listening. Yuh. What*ever*.

---

[96] Presumably to scrape the poo off with.
[97] The inspiration, obviously, for the teddy bear – although they're usually produced without the historically accurate club marks.

The Astronomer

Quick Reading

Far out, beyond the orbit of the Moon, past the arseteroid belt, you will find yourself illuminated by the rings of Uranus.[98]

 Rites of Passage

Calm & Serene

Accept your place in the grand scheme of things and let the stuff of life flow over you.

Sound & Fury

Spend too long contemplating the infinite and you'll find that you're in very real danger of disappearing into your own black hole.

What Did You Eat?

The universe may be infinite but the explanation for your ice-cream-cone-shaped shite is very down to earth. Cut down on the 99s and take the time to have a decent meal once in a while.

---

[98] Come on, you knew it was going to be in this book *somewhere*.

 **Detailed Reading**

Look up at the night sky and you will be overwhelmed by the scale of it all. It's humbling to think just how small we are in the grand scheme of things, and yet this knowledge is key to our growth as human beings. Only by recognising that we are part of a larger whole can we transcend our petty concerns, fulfil our destiny and stop dropping such strangely shaped turds into the toilet bowl.

But, though we strive to eliminate such base excretions, we must recognise that, since the dawn of time, all matter has been recycled from the initial debris of the Big Bang. Put plainly, we are all made of stardust. Remember that when you're stuck on a bus or arguing over how to split a restaurant bill. Ashes to ashes, dust to dust, if boredom don't get you, wanky New Age bullshit must.

Sorry, but we're really not comfortable with all this 'it is written in the stars' stuff because we all know the truth – it's written in your shit. Don't get us wrong – an understanding of the larger picture is good, but try not to get too lost in the mysteries of the cosmos. The Astronomer studies the stars, but a wise man keeps an eye on botty products.

What Action Can I Take?

Well, you could start by pulling your head out of your arse and paying some attention to the world around you rather than floating off on flights of fancy. There. See what you've done? You've made us alliterate.

The Astronomer is a clear and certain sign that you're spending too much time contemplating the infinite and not enough time on everyday matters. Sure, the world's a bit of a mess at the moment and things may well get worse before they get better. But, if you think you can spend the bad times losing yourself in the vastness of space and head back to Earth the minute things take an upturn, then you're part of the problem instead of being part of the solution.

To put it more bluntly: it's your shit, you shovel it.

Historical Context

If it's people with too much on their mind you're after, what better historical exemplar than the man who has variously been called 'the father of modern observational astronomy', 'the father of modern physics' and 'the father of modern science'? So who's the swot with too much brain for one head? None other than Galileo Galilei.

The Italian genius made improvements to the telescope and compass, discovered the four largest moons of Jupiter and championed the heliocentric view of the universe – until the kindly holy men of the Church threatened him with torture unless he recanted his views.

Galileo's most relevant experiment (as far as Arsetrologers are concerned) took place when he dropped two shits of equal weight but differing shapes and sizes from the top

The Astronomer

of the Leaning Tower of Pisa. He was attempting to prove that, regardless of how big a turd is, the distance the bits of corn are flung when it hits the ground remains constant. Or something like that.

Inverted

How appropriate, particularly given the nature of the historical personage most closely linked with The Astronomer, that when you invert this rune it gives you The Dunce.

The interesting[99] thing about The Dunce is that the effect of the rune is almost exactly the same as the effect of The Astronomer – but the forces behind it are completely different. If you've dropped The Dunce, you are every bit as prone to removing yourself from the world around you, to the detriment of many (including yourself). But unlike with crappers of The Astronomer, it's not the infinite vastness of space in which you've lost yourself: it's your own navel.

Yes, while better and brighter men than you contemplate the great mysteries of the universe, you are content to sit on the floor in your birthday suit vainly trying to establish whether or not you can produce a fart of sufficient power to make your balls move. You can't. Trust us.[100]

---

[99] And we use the word 'interesting' in its very loosest sense.
[100] Who says we don't do research?

The Phantom

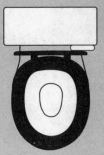

Quick Reading

You felt the movement, the change in air pressure and the unmistakable presence in the room. But, when you look, there's nothing there!

 Rites of Passage

Calm & Serene

There is more to the world than what can be seen or touched. Namely, smelly things hiding out of sight.

Sound & Fury

Is your house haunted by a poltergeist – or is there something else making the toilet door rattle?

What Did You Eat?

It's somewhat academic, given that the poo in question has vanished without a trace. You could have chowed down on swan, sherbet or shami kebab and it wouldn't make the slightest bit of difference, as the evidence has disappeared from your bowl. We could speculate as to what makes the phenomenon of the ghost poo possible, but we like to maintain the air of mystery that surrounds it. In other words, we don't know. Or, to put it in a way that doesn't fundamentally compromise the integrity of our mission, the reasons are purely spiritual and nothing to do with the mundane process of digestion.

 **Detailed Reading**

Strange noises are often disconcerting, but the appearance
– or rather *disappearance* – of The Phantom is a grim omen
indeed. Consider it a warning, a sign that you will soon be
visited by some powerful spirits. No, not spirits – what's the
word we're looking for? Gas. That's it.

The Phantom is a sure and sorry sign that you've taken your
last solid dump for a while and a time of unbridled flatulence
is soon to be visited upon you. Think of it as being like
Marley visiting Scrooge – a precursor to the main event, but
still pretty frightening whichever way you look at it.

You can get ready for this visitation in one of two ways. You
can either hide under the bed and close your eyes, hoping to
avoid the inevitable, or you can stand up and face whatever
is coming your way. Like a man. Like a very loud, smelly man.

So, what's it to be? Heard but unseen? Or loud and proud?

 What Action Can I Take?

To be honest, there's not a lot to choose between the two
options above. If you take the second path, you walk out
into the world, stand tall, keep your chin up and let rip
obstreperously and frequently. Result? Let's just say you
won't be needing to spend so much time accepting friends
on Facebook.

Then the first strategy is better? Well, not really. Put it this
way: the last time you were a kid and your brother used
to fart in his bed, force you under the bedclothes and hold
you there until you started coughing – was that a good
experience or a bad one?

♎ Historical Context

Much as we'd dearly love to claim that the creator of Sherlock Holmes was a farter of prodigious strength and frequency, we're afraid that Sir Arthur Conan Doyle makes it into this section mainly for his credulous attitude to the spirit world rather than any hitherto unrevealed penchant for cutting the cheese.

Conan Doyle was an avid spiritualist, believing in the afterlife, fairies, communing with the dead and all manner of supernatural phenomena. He was great friends with Harry Houdini, who he was convinced was himself possessed of supernatural abilities. Thus the thematic link to The Phantom.

The good doctor is, of course, best known for creating the legendary detective Sherlock Holmes, but he also penned a number of stories about the scientific adventurer Professor Challenger. The most famous of these was the novel *The Lost World*, in which an expedition discovers a land where time has stood still and dinosaurs walk the earth.

It's this that makes Conan Doyle a fine match for the Arsetrological meaning of The Phantom. All manner of dinosaurs walked the Lost World, including the brontosaurus – and, if anything can shake the earth with its arse trumpets, it must be an animal that weighs the same as four elephants and eats nothing but vegetables.

The Phantom

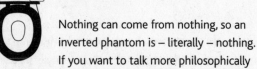

Inverted

Nothing can come from nothing, so an inverted phantom is – literally – nothing. If you want to talk more philosophically about what the inverse of nothing is, then we'd be happy to engage in a lengthy dialectic about the nature of reality. Unfortunately, this is a book and, if you're expecting a conversation with a printed page, you're quite clearly a fucking nutter. But wait! Maybe it's not your fault. It could be that the spirit of the Phantom has got hold of you and you are currently channelling voices from the ether.

Wait! Hang on! If you're hearing voices and talking to books . . . No, we had it right first time – you've gone round the twist.

The Succubus

Quick Reading

A woman forces you into unusual positions. No, not in *that* way! Down, boy!

Rites of Passage

Calm & Serene

Relax and enjoy yourself. There can be no pleasure without pain.

Sound & Fury

But it's hard to breathe when you've got a ball gag in your mouth.

🍔 What Did You Eat?

According to leading Arsetrological authorities,[101] there is no known dietary intake that can explain this particular rune. It arises solely from a specific alignment of karmic forces – namely, your face forced onto the ground by the stiletto heel of a leather boot. What did you eat? You ate whatever Mistress gave you permission to eat, that's what!

---

[101] Namely us.

# Detailed Reading

A domineering woman forcing you into uncomfortable positions might sound good if you're of a slightly kinky persuasion, but this isn't a bit of saucy fun we're talking about: this is the evil power of The Succubus.

This rune is a clear sign that you are being manipulated by a woman in your life. It's probably someone very close to you, although you may well find that the malign influence is coming from a woman a remove or two from your intimate circle.[102] Look around you to see what's different. Is a woman close to you becoming Machiavellian and confusing to be around? Or has something else changed and you've only just woken up to it? Exactly how long is it since you've seen your best mate? Isn't it odd that his wife always seems to have 'planned something else'? All right, so you got drunk at her birthday, insulted her sweaty friend and tried to get off with her, but you would have thought she could get past *that* minor indiscretion.

What we're saying is take a good look at the women in your life. One of them is out to suck you dry. And not in an exciting mostly-fictional-letter-to-*Penthouse*-forum way, either.

What Action Can I Take?

This is a very difficult question. The Succubus must be approached with caution. You can't just leap into the fray: you need a strategy. When dealing with The Succubus at a remove, great care and subtlety are required. You cannot ask your best friend to choose between his significant other and

---

[102] What? You're looking at us as if you're expecting something . . .

you, for you will lose. (For sure. Check out the tits on her! *You'd* sacrifice you for her.) You must manoeuvre events to such a place that your friend has no option but to see the scheming of his partner laid bare.

If The Succubus is close to you, the danger is greater but the degree of interpersonal politics required is smaller. Once you've identified the danger, there's no point beating about the bush. You may as well just confront the demon and have done with it. No, the danger here is not physical but sexual. You may start with the intention of breaking things off, but all thoughts of ending the relationship will go out the window once she replies, 'I'm so sorry you feel that way. I feel terrible that I've put you through such pain. Why don't we discuss it further after I've given you a deep muscle massage and a blow job so powerful it will suck the bedclothes up through your arse?'

Your best defence against The Succubus is to make yourself thoroughly unattractive to her. We'd suggest the truth: 'I'm sorry, but I think it's time we went our separate ways. You see, I've studied my shit and it tells me you're the Devil.' If the girl's got any sense, she'll run a mile.

Historical Context

If we ignore the many and varied examples in mythology and demonology, and stick strictly to history, we quickly find that the most appropriate personification of The Succubus is Margaretha Geertruida Zelle – better known to the world at large as Mata Hari.

Mata Hari – exotic dancer, courtesan and spy during the First World War – was the original *femme fatale*, the prototype from whom all other scarlet women are descended. Well, not *literally* descended; we mean descended in a titular[103] sense. The thought of a seductive temptress, operating as a double agent and using her feminine wiles to extract top-secret information from military targets caught the popular imagination of the time. It's quite likely, though, that she was never more than an opportunist, who invented stories of espionage to make her life sound more exotic. Hence her suitability for The Succubus – single-minded and seductive but, ultimately, full of shit.

Inverted

As you may have noticed, the shape of the succubus is two rounded forms in the upper half, signifying the breasts, and a lower thatch to signify the . . . lower thatch. Needless to say, if you invert the rune the bulbous bags hang at the bottom, while rising to an upward point. As anyone who's ever drawn a willy on a maths exercise book will tell you, this is as close an approximation to the male genitalia as art or science has ever accomplished, and therefore we have a rather convenient parallel between the male and female forms.

But these aren't any normal male and female we're talking about. No, to find the Succubus's male counterpart, we have to look for a male who preys upon women in the same single-minded way. A tasteless, classless, remorseless prick on legs. Therefore we name this libidinous inverted rune, The Lothario – a symbol of what happens when the prick meets the shit.

---

[103] You know, this word is used quite incorrectly. But under the circumstances, I'm inclined to let it stand. – Ed.

The Magi

Quick Reading

Wise men come bearing gifts, but they also bring high expectations.

 Rites of Passage

Calm & Serene

Everyone likes a nice prezzie now and then, but such bountiful gifts when it's not even your birthday make you feel a little uncomfortable.

Sound & Fury

Sometimes it's easy to get carried away by the decorations and frills surrounding the issue. A turd is still a turd, no matter how beautifully it's wrapped.

🍔 What Did You Eat?

There's an obvious link to Christmas here, so we're looking at one of two options. Either your intestines are groaning under the weight of turkey, stuffing, roast potatoes, Yorkshire pud, carrots, swede, Christmas cake, Christmas pudding, mince pies, brandy butter (and any number of other seasonal treats too rich to eat all year round) and have fired out these three nuggets as warning shots before the rest comes tumbling out, or your body has somehow managed to let three Brussels sprouts pass through your body without digesting (or hopefully even tasting) them.

Detailed Reading

The parallels between this rune and the Nativity might get you excited, but let's get one thing clear from the offset: you're not the Messiah, you're not even just a very naughty boy. You're a grubby little man who buys books about poo, so let's get any delusions of grandeur out of our minds, shall we?

No, we're afraid the only remotely religious aspect of The Magi is that it is meant to be read as a parable, not as direct experience. So it's quite possible that the gifts you receive will come from three men, but whether they are actually wise is neither here nor there. What is important is the fact that they're giving you presents – not because they think you deserve them, not even because they like you, but because they believe you have something that's of value to them. Whether that something is knowledge, contacts or the fact that you have a swimming pool, the sad truth is that these aren't so much gifts as down payments. Altogether now: 'I do you this favour out of friendship. One day – and that day may never come – I will ask you to do a favour for me'.

In summary, and in the finest traditions of the Corleone family, these three 'kings' are expecting a return on their investment. Bear that in mind before you accept their gifts – they may end up costing you in the end.

What Action Can I Take?

As with so many of these runes, the watchword here is caution. Be aware of what's going on around you – and especially aware of sudden admirers. If you keep your wits about you, you should be able to spot these false friends coming from a mile away.

Mind you, that's easier said than done. You try keeping your attention focused on anything but your own discomfort while the smallest room in the house is echoing with the report of three 50-calibre rounds being fired out of your arse into the bowl, and you're trying to cope with the shock of your ringpiece recoiling up into your bowels. Napalm in the morning may smell like victory, but the aftermath of passing The Magi will leave a very different aroma. So, what can you do? Holding your breath might be a good start.

Of course, if we were to continue the *Godfather* imagery from above, the logical course of action would no doubt involve horses' heads or the taking of hostages. But we're not going to continue in that vein because we take the . . . message . . . we received in the post this morning seriously. Very seriously. We're sorry. We meant no disrespect.

Please don't hurt us.

Historical Context

It was tempting here to choose Richard Neville, Earl of Warwick during the Wars of the Roses and known to all as the 'Kingmaker'. After all, if your criterion is someone who bears luxurious gifts but with strings attached, you can't get much more appropriate. After careful consideration, though, we thought, Why look a gift shite in the bum? If the runes provide us with The Magi, then the Magi we shall have.

The word 'magi' has many meanings depending on what source you consult. It could mean astrologers, magicians, inventors, but the meaning we're most common with, these days, comes from the Bible: wise men.

The Magi were reputed to be the three wise men who followed a star in order to drop in on the infant Jesus Christ, in a stable in Bethlehem. According to Western tradition, their names were Caspar, Melchior and Balthasar, so it's unsurprising that they were referred to as 'Magi'. If we were them, *we'd* be desperate for a collective noun, too. The gifts they brought to present to the baby Jesus were, of course, gold, frankincense and myrrh, which are particularly appropriate to students of Arsetrology: gold to buy new nappies with, frankincense to cover up the smell of poo and myrrh to use as an antiseptic balm on the sore botty bits.

Inverted

If we look at the opposite of wisdom, we get stupidity and so it's easy enough to see the Magi's doppelgängers as being The Three Stooges. Given that The Magi is one of those runes of which it's difficult to tell whether they're the right way up, identifying it as inverted is, in this case, down to you. Everyone knows Larry, Curley and Moe, but before now had you ever heard of Caspar, Melchior and Balthasar? We thought not. So, if you find yourself naming the three little scamps swimming in your private pond, take it as read that those aren't wise men you're looking at.

Conclusion

So, what have we learned?

First, we've learned that there are all sorts of things that our shit can tell us. It can tell us about our hopes, our dreams, our aspirations and our fears. By staring our droppings in the face, we're able to get a better understanding of who we are as people and what we're looking for in the world. The fact that we strive for truth, for meaning and for some sense of something larger than ourselves is what makes us great. We may be looking for answers in all the wrong places, but it's the quest for enlightenment that makes us truly divine.[104]

Second, we suppose we've learned that, no matter how bizarre and seemingly random the shape of your shit might be, there's always some sick puppy out there who can not only see a pattern in it, but is quite willing to assign meaning and a higher purpose to it and even suggest you should attempt to live your life according to its dictates. If it weren't for the fact that that also accurately describes what 99 per cent of the world's religions are up to, we'd be appalled. (But not so appalled that we're not prepared to exploit the desperate lengths people will go to for answers.) If we've plumbed some depths that perhaps should have been left alone, we can only apologise.

Above all, we've learned that for all the manifold names for the end-product of the digestive system, for all the spiritual mumbo-jumbo and the desperate *double entendres*, the imagination, the redolence, the humour and even the occasional onomatopoeia of the more inventive names, it's

---

[104] That's 'divine' as in 'holy'; not 'Divine' as in the drag-queen actor who ate a piece of dog poo in the bad-taste movie *Pink Flamingos*. Although . . .

very difficult to top the simple childish humour of the word 'poo' for laugh value.

And that's it from us. We hope you've found this little tour through Turdsville both amusing and illuminating and that we've helped you all get your shit together.

Thanks, everyone, and don't forget to flush.